Chinatown

Boise, Idaho, 1870–1970

唐人埠

Chinatown

Boise, Idaho, 1870–1970

貝市埠

Arthur A. Hart

Historic Idaho, Inc.
Boise, Idaho

Published by Historic Idaho, Inc.
P.O. Box 4534
Boise, ID 83711
Tel. (208) 375-2092 or 342-7929

Printed in the United States of America.

Historic Idaho is a non-profit organization dedicated to the publication of books about Idaho's history, people, and culture.

IBN 0-9705453-0-4

Photo credits include ISHS for Idaho State Historical Society. The Society has graciously granted use of its materials to further its own statutory responsibilities and the objectives of Historic Idaho, Inc., a 501c3 Non-profit.

Dedication

To Idaho's Chinese pioneers and their American descendants who continue to contribute to our cultural and economic advancement.

Table of Contents

Introduction

I began my research on the Chinese in Boise in 1969 shortly after I returned to Idaho and began my work at the Idaho State Historical Society. Surviving from the city's once thriving Chinatown were the Hip Sing Tong and the Hop Sing Tong buildings, near the corner of Front Street and Capitol Boulevard. They were soon to be demolished as part of the city's urban renewal project. The full historic significance of these buildings and their contents could only be realized at some future date when there was the time and necessary expertise available to study them in detail. The decision was made to move everything to the society's storage facility—truckloads of artifacts, printed materials, and photographs. I'll tell more about these collections later.

The historian writing an account of Boise's Chinatown must of necessity rely heavily on newspaper reports of the time. These reflect reporters' prejudice and ignorance of Chinese culture, but as contemporary accounts they are generally accurate as to time and place. The bias shown is, of course, an important part of the story. Words used for the Chinese, such as "Celestial," "Mongolian," "Oriental," "Chinaman," "heathen," and "John," are today considered offensive, but their use is unavoidable when quoting from accounts of the time. Even Caucasians sympathetic to the plight of the Chinese making their way in an alien and unfriendly land resorted to the use of some of those names. The word "Celestial" came into use because China in the 18th and 19th centuries styled itself the Celestial Empire, with the implication that its emperors ruled on the throne of heaven by divine right. The words "Chinaman" and "Oriental," considered offensive today, probably weren't thought so by Idaho's Chinese pioneers themselves who—used "Melican Man" to parallel "Chinaman" and had far bigger problems of racial discrimination than the names they were called in the newspapers.

I have benefited from recently published material on the history of the Chinese in Idaho and am grateful for the work of Liping Zhu, whose book *A Chinaman's Chance* gives balance to the perception fostered by most works on the Chinese that they were a brutally treated and downtrodden minority. He points out that they accomplished what they came for and that indeed America gave them a chance. The vast majority did make money and did return home rich by Chinese standards of the time. By coming to America they escaped wretched conditions in poverty-stricken Guangdong province, from which nearly all of them came, and by sending money home they were able to improve the lives of their families there. At the same time they made a significant contribution to the American economy by building railroads, mining, farming, and working in whatever other industries needed their labor.

Priscilla Wegars's *Chinese at the Confluence* is a compact overview of the Chinese experience in Idaho and particularly of Lewiston's Chinese history. Her work on the archaeology of Chinese sites in Idaho, and as curator of the Alfred W. Bowers Laboratory of Anthropology's Asian American Comparative Collection at the University of Idaho, is a significant contribution.

There is a vast literature on the history of the Chinese in the American West, but the Idaho material deals almost exclusively with mining. The internet is an invaluable source of information on Chinatowns in a dozen other American and Canadian cities, useful for giving perspective and context for what happened in Boise.

Oral history interviews, conducted first by Jackie Day-Ames in 1976 and by the author in 2001 and 2002, allowed descendants of pioneer Chinese in Boise to tell their own family stories. Day-Ames also interviewed elderly Caucasians whose memories extended back into the late 19th century. These informants are no longer living, but their perceptions of the Chinese are valuable social documents. Day-Ames's interviews with the late Mabel Quong are a poignant revelation of the courage it took for a young Chinese girl to come to America, to cope with an alien society, to marry and raise a large family, and to start a strawberry farm that would prosper through her hard work and perseverance.

I am indebted to the following members of pioneer families for their time and encouragement as this book was being researched and written: First, To Andy Louie, for many hours of patient collaboration, for sharing family photographs, and for creating the beautiful calligraphy that adorns the book's chapter headings; to Dick Ah Fong, great-grandson of C.K. Ah Fong, for his friendship and early interest in the Historical Society's efforts to preserve Boise's Chinese history; to Faye Yee and her children for sharing memories and photographs of herbalist Yick Yee. Thank you, Sue, Jane, Grant and Boyd; to Bill Quong, son of Mabel and Louie Quong; to Raymond Fong, son of Harry and Gretta Fong, for his good will, and to Chong Yip (Godfrey) for translations and explanations of religious practices in Guangdong brought to America. My thanks to Helen Thompson for allowing me to read the unpublished manuscript of her book on the Louie family, *Slow Boat From China.*

As always I relied heavily on the resources of the Idaho State Historical Society library and archives. Judith Austin, Carolyn S. Bowler, Kathy Hodges, Larry Jones, Linda Morton-Keithley, and John Yandell all directed me to materials I needed. My dear friend and colleague Merle W. Wells gave valuable suggestions in the early stages of this project and up to the last days of his life. Merle's encouragement and vast knowledge were shared generously with all who asked.

The materials from the Hip Sing Building mentioned earlier received their first expert analysis in 1979 by two scholars interested in Chinese medicine. Paul D. Buell and Christopher Muench researched the Ah Fong family medical practice, founded by Dr. C.K. Ah Fong, and carried on by his son Herbert and grandson Gerald. (The Ah Fong's story can be found in the chapter on Chinese doctors.) Their study revealed that the Ah Fong pharmacy was a veritable time capsule of traditional Chinese medical practice, no longer to be found in modern China. Their findings were published in the *Annals of the Chinese Historical Society of the Pacific Northwest* in 1983 and by Seattle's Wing Luke Memorial Museum in 1984.

In 1988 and 1989 intern Li-hua Yu from Bowling Green University cataloged the entire Hip Sing collection, comprised of artifacts, books, documents, financial records, correspondence, magazines, newspapers, and photographs. Her translations revealed among other things a Chinese library, not only of medical books dating from the 1860s, but of ancient classics, some printed in the 18th century. There are many records of the Hip Sing Tong, the earliest dated 1924, the last from the early 1950s. Li-hua Yu's dissertation, based on her work in Boise, reveals much about the last years of the benevolent and protective societies before Chinatown virtually ceased to exist.

Bruce Edward Hall's *Tea That Burns: A Family Memoir of Chinatown* was useful in confirming the similarities of Chinese experience and culture in a great eastern city and a small western one. New York City's Chinese community had the same problems to deal with as Boise's—working around the Exclusion Acts, avoiding clashes between powerful tongs that led to bloodshed in both cities (both had a branch of the Hip Sing Tong), and cultivating friendships with local politicians and the police.

Last, but first in all we share, I wish to acknowledge the contributions of my wife Novella D, who is my editor, counselor, word-processing expert, and, when necessary, taskmaster. Her dedication to "getting this thing over with" was what ultimately did. She could sympathize with the little girl who wrote in a book report: "This book told me more than I cared to know about Indians." We hope, gentle reader, that this book will make you want to know *more* about Boise's Chinese history. This, at least, is a start.

Arthur A. Hart
Boise, Idaho, 2002

I

The Chinese Come to Idaho

到達中國人

Boise's Chinese pioneers preferred the traditional clothing of their homeland. This man is wearing his best outfit for the photographer.
ISHS 75-124.22

"That interesting sight so familiar to old Californians of long trains of Celestials on the move in single file, supporting the middle of their long handled shovels or bamboo stick with pendant sacks of rice, chop sticks, rockers, and gum boots, filed along Idaho Street yesterday morning to the great amusement of lookers on. Some dusty pilgrims [recent white arrivals] eyed the Johns with great curiosity, as it was their first introduction to the inhabitants of the Flowery Kingdom."[1]

The September, 1865, news item above was headlined "John's First Appearance," so we can assume that these were indeed the first Chinese to pass through Boise

Louie Kong was one of a large number of men of the Louie family who worked in Boise in the 19th century. In his part of Guangdong province there are dozens of villages where everyone is named Louie.
ISHS SG 26/117

on their way to the mines in Boise Basin, roughly 40 miles to the northeast. They had come from Nevada, walking all the way. Forty-nine Chinese were killed by Indians in June of 1866 near the Owyhee River crossing southwest of Silver City. Only one survived to tell the story. These Chinese had a few horses, but most were on foot. Later arrivals in Boise Basin came by stagecoach.[2] The *Portland Oregonian* had reported in February, 1865: "According to the testimony of the Chinese agents, a very large immigration of Chinese miners may be expected in the Upper Country the coming season. They variously estimate the number from 2000 to 5000."[3] The first of these, "to the number of 15 to 20" arrived in Walla Walla in February of 1865 "on their way to the Snake River and Oro Fino mines. They say 'heap more Johns

It was a rare and fortunate Chinese man in early Boise who had a wife. A few in that 95-percent male society had wives and families in China but could not bring them to America.
ISHS 63-203.1

come velly soon; not know how much; but heap steamboat bling 'em.'"[4]

Chinese merchants were among the first to arrive in Boise Basin and were well established there by September of 1865. The *Idaho World* wrote "The Chinamen are coming among us. Lord deliver us from the 'Locusts of Egypt.' They devour all before them. If destiny has so shaped it, let them come." In the same issue it noted the shooting of a Chinese and said "The Chinese in Idaho are very harmless and very industrious and I will venture to say that such is not the character of the man, whoever he is, that kills one of them without provocation . . . . To kill a Chinaman or a defenseless woman, or to strangle a canary bird—one is about as brave as another."[5]

Mark Twain echoed the sentiments of the *World* when he wrote of the Chinese: "They are a kindly-disposed, well-meaning race, and are respected and well

**Teen-age Gwong Louie was an avid baseball fan.
He was described by the *Idaho Statesman* in 1893 as
"the versatile young Chinese known all over the city."
He inscribed this portrait to his Boise elementary school teacher.**
ISHS 2159

treated by the upper classes, all over the Pacific coast. No Californian gentleman or lady ever abuses or oppresses a Chinaman, under any circumstance . . . only the scum of the population do it—they and their children; they, and, naturally and consistently, the policemen and politicians, likewise, for these are the dust-licking pimps and slaves of the scum . . . ."[6]

When the Chinese were well established in Boise in their Idaho Street Chinatown in 1877 William Bollard, rector of St. Michael's Episcopal Church, wrote: "Of the population [of Boise City] about 100 are Chinese. They are quiet and industrious and generally engaged in household service or in the laundry business. Their wages as servants vary from $5 to $8 per week."[7]

As with all immigrants to America in the 19th century, the Chinese had to take whatever work they could get. They had come here as sojourners, intending to stay only long enough to earn money to help their families and to return to them with what would seem a fortune in the poverty-stricken province of Guangdong (Kwantung). Some had wives and children or elderly parents that needed help at home, but in America they were a bachelor society. They lived lonely lives, longing for the day when they could return to the land of their ancestors. They created small cultural enclaves that reminded them of home, in what was often a hostile environment. Their needs were soon met by Chinese merchants who imported goods from home, especially rice, tea, and other staples of the peasant diet.

Every western Chinatown, including Boise's, had a temple where traditional gods were worshiped. Every Chinese hoped to be buried with his ancestors. If he died in America his bones were shipped back to China. Most elderly Chinese returned to their native villages to die, secure in the knowledge that their families would perform the final rites dictated by tradition thousands of years old.

In 1870, when the first federal census for Idaho was taken 4,274 Chinese were counted—most of them in Boise Basin. By 1880 about a thousand had left, many settling in Boise, others continuing on to California or

This enhanced detail from an 1884 fire map of Boise shows the location of the city's first Chinatown. In addition to several structures labeled "Dwg" for "Dwelling," note the "Chinese Gambling Ho." (house) in the cluster of buildings at upper right.

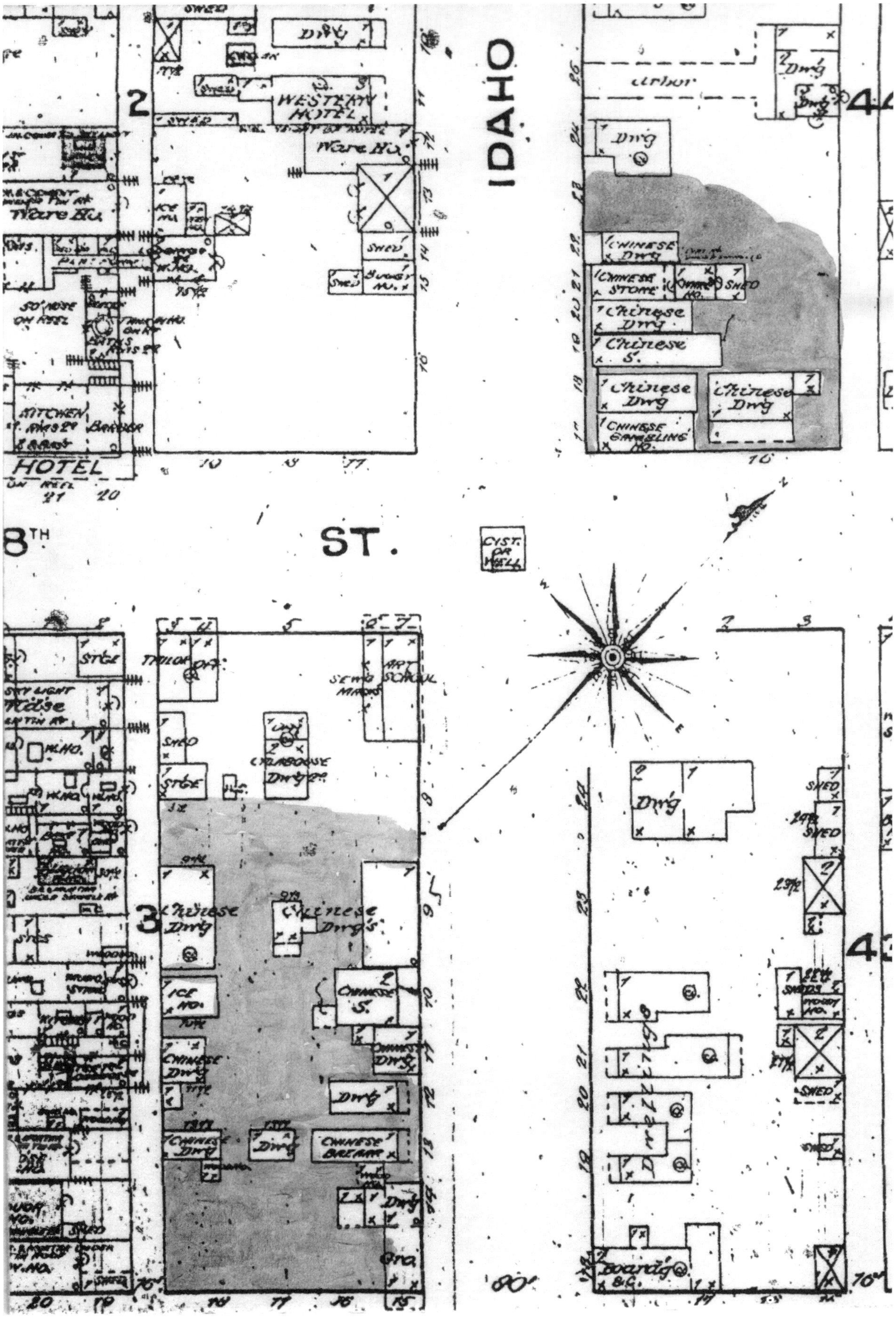
IDAHO
8TH
ST.
HOTEL
WESTERN HOTEL
Ware Ho.
Dwg
arbor
CHINESE Dwg
CHINESE STORE
Chinese Dwg
Chinese S.
CHINESE GAMBLING HO.
CYST. OR WELL
TAILOR
SEWG MACH.
ART SCHOOL
CALABOOSE Dwg
Chinese Dwg
Chinese Dwg's
ICE HO.
CHINESE S.
CHINESE Dwg
CHINESE BREAD
Boardg & C.
SHED
STGE
2
3
43
44

back to China. The 1890 census listed 2,007, and by 1900 there were 1,467. The Chinese population of Idaho continued to drop to 859 in 1910 and to only 585 in 1920. Most of the sojourners had fulfilled their dream and returned home.[8]

II

Religion

宗教

Chinese religious festivals on the streets of Boise always attracted large crowds of curious citizens. The smoke of exploding firecrackers creates a background for this dancing figure at Seventh and Front streets.
ISHS 60-52.404

Chinese tolerance and acceptance of new religions over the centuries grew into a layered system of beliefs that included Confucianism, Taoism, Buddhism, ancestor worship, and the belief that all natural objects had spirits of their own. Much of the emphasis in religious ceremonies was on warding off evil spirits and on seeking good fortune. Firecrackers, a part of every celebration including funerals, were believed to frighten away evil spirits, including the spirits of the dead who might come back to torment the living. Good luck charms were important too, especially to the substantial number of Chinese who loved to gamble.[1] To most Caucasian Boiseans, these and other Chinese religious observances were baffling and usually considered amusing. Reverence for ancestors, expressed by leaving offerings at tombs, and other aspects of Chinese religion were not understood by members of the white community. Had they known more about their exotic neighbors' beliefs, they might have shown more respect for them, but the language barrier effectively prevented understanding.

Chinese New Year's parades were colorful annual events looked forward to by the entire community. This procession on Seventh Street has just crossed Main Street. The buildings in the immediate background are still there, minus the porch.
ISHS 68-14.l

Buddhism came to China from India in the early years of the Christian Era. The teaching of Siddhartha Gautama Buddha, born south of the Himalayas about 563 B.C., center around the Four Noble Truths: Life is filled with suffering; suffering is caused by people's wants; suffering can be ended if people stop wanting things, such as more pleasure, wealth, or power. To stop wanting things, people must follow eight basic laws. These are: To know the truth, to intend to resist evil, to say nothing to hurt others, to respect life, property, and morality, to work at a job that does not injure others, to try to free one's mind from evil, to be in control of one's feelings and thoughts, to practice the appropriate forms of concentration.[2]

A Buddhist proverb says: *Hatred can never overcome hatred in this world. Love alone can overcome hatred.* This philosophy, coupled with the teachings and proverbs of Confucius, born in China within a few years of Buddha, helps explain the long-suffering patience of the Chinese in the New World in the face of bigotry, persecution, and

Whole roast pig was a favorite dish on special occasions. This 1897 snapshot shows a Chinese man offering hospitality to two curious whites. Ramshackle buildings like those in the background were typical of Boise's Idaho Street Chinatown.
ISHS 72-98.105

occasional violence.[3] It now seems clear that racial prejudice gradually lessened over time, and that through their own conduct and conciliatory efforts Boise's Chinese came to be regarded as an enriching element in the city's life. They contributed to worthy causes, took part in Fourth of July parades, and went out of their way to be viewed as good American citizens. Boiseans enjoyed Chinese festivals and celebrations and many of them were invited to be guests for special quasi-religious events like christenings and weddings. When Chinese adopted Christianity and western customs and dress, they were editorially praised in the newspapers for becoming "better Americans." In the struggle for survival, minorities have often had to take on protective coloration, and nobody did so better than the Chinese.[4]

Early newspaper stories often referred to the Chinese as "heathen," though their ethical and moral philosophy predated the teachings of Christ by many centuries. Confucius (551–479 BC) became China's dominant philosopher, both morally and politically, and has continued to be so many centuries after his death.

Some Boise families still honor ancestors in rural Guangdong, China, by leaving offerings of food on their graves. After this gesture of love and respect is made, the food is eaten at a special banquet of celebration of the lives of the departed.
Courtesy Andy Louie

His writings defined the obligations of people to each other: husband-wife, parent-child, ruler-subjects, which, if followed faithfully could bring about a just and harmonious society.[5] It was Confucius who first wrote: "Do not do unto others what you would not like yourself," the earliest recorded expression of the golden rule. This appeared in the New Testament in Matthew 7:12 as "Whatsoever ye would that men should do to you, do ye even so to them," and in Luke 6:31 as "And as ye would that men should do to you, do ye also to them likewise."[6]

Boise's Chinatown was the largest in the intermountain area by the 1880s, and Chinese from other towns came to join in religious celebrations. Chief among these was the lunar New Year. A lunar month is the 29½ days it takes for the moon to complete its orbit around the earth. In the Chinese calendar the lunar year is 11 days shorter than our solar year. To make up the difference the Chinese add seven lunar months every 19 years. That is why the Chinese New Year's celebration begins on a different date each year, anywhere between January 21 and February 19.[7]

The lion dancer was a favorite at every Chinese parade. Despite the photographer's label on this 1896 photograph, this is a lion, not a dragon. The lion opened his huge mouth to receive offerings of coins as he cavorted along the street.
ISHS 77-148.2

The lion was the comic in Chinese New Year's parades. He was tormented by a clown who danced around him. Children loved it.
ISHS SG 26/20

As this lion dance photo shows, it only took one man to carry his head and trail his body. The dragon needed several bearers to bring him to life.
ISHS 76-18.9

The arrival of the New Year is seen by the Chinese as well as westerners as a time for a fresh start. Debts are paid, new clothes are worn, and houses and places of business get a general cleaning. Families and friends meet to feast and give thanks for the blessings enjoyed in the year past and to pray for good fortune in the year ahead. Ancestors are honored and presents are given to children.[8] In Boise and nearby mining towns like Idaho City, there were virtually no Chinese children, but many in the city's more than 90 percent male Chinese society had wives and children in China. Young unmarried men hoped, and no doubt prayed to the gods, that they might return to their native land and find a bride. The New Year's celebration in Boise's Chinese community was such a colorful and noisy event that it was written about in the newspapers every year. Firecrackers imported from China were exploded by the thousands to drive away evil spirits. In 1877 the *Statesman* said: "The celebration consists mainly in having a big time, lots of good things to eat, drink, and smoke. An incessant roar will be

The parade dragon was displayed in all his glory on a series of stands before being taken up by his seven bearers.
ISHS photo

This parade dragon, photographed near Seventh and Main, has a distinctly fierce look and very sharp teeth. The lion, by comparison, is more a figure of fun. In this photo he is nearly hidden by the men at far left.
ISHS 72-201.117

The Chinese contributed this horse-drawn dragon float to a Fourth of July parade around the year 1900. Note the huge silk dragon flag being carried past the Overland Hotel at Eighth and Main—a building that was torn down in 1905.
ISHS 76-138.84

kept up nightly during the week so that Josh may know that his children are properly worshiping him."[9]

The *Idaho World* wrote about Chinese New Year's hospitality toward the white community in Idaho City in 1885 in words that could equally apply to the celebration in Boise: "The Chinese are very hospitable on their holidays, and treat those of the 'Melican' race who call on them with the best they have, and are always pleased to receive calls."[10]

Although the traditional New Year's celebration in China lasted two weeks, by 1890 Boise's was about a

The Chinese played a major part in this Fourth of July parade, shown here passing the corner of Eleventh and Main. From the style of clothing worn by women onlookers, we date this photo to about 1916.
ISHS 81-20.4

week. Describing the significance of the holiday to the Chinese, the *Statesman* wrote "Much of the time during these days will be devoted to visiting from house to house and in feasting upon whatever dainties and delicacies the Chinese stores and markets can supply. In the exchange of presents and hospitalities the outside barbarian is not forgotten, as the Chinaman manages always to remember all his friends of whatever race or nationality."[11]

At the turn of the century complaints from citizens about the incessant explosion of firecrackers at night led Mayor J.H. Richards to limit their use to between the hours of seven and midnight.[12] In February 1901, the paper said: "In America, at least, there are thousands who feel very thankful that New Year for the Chinese comes but once a year."[13] It was also observed that year that "the Chinese New Year is certainly a day of good will."[14]

The 1911 celebration in Boise attracted Chinese from Pocatello, Silver City, and Baker, Oregon. There were 30 from Idaho City and 15 from LaGrande, Oregon.[15] In 1912 the Chinese applied formally to the City Council for permission to shoot fireworks at an early hour in the morning to usher in their New Year. The Chief of Police was told to use his own discretion.[16]

In the 1920s great banquets to which prominent white guests were invited were held by the Chinese associations. In 1926 the Soo Yuen club, family organization of the Fongs, Louies, and Kwongs, seated 175 guests, the Hip Sing Tong 50, and the Hop Sing Tong 75. The Chinese Masons held their feast in new quarters on Front Street.[17]

By that time, nostalgia for Chinatown's "good old days" had crept into each year's account of the New Year's celebration. Especially missed were the colorful parades of the 1910s in which scores of Chinese men in their finest silken clothing carried banners from the temples, Chinese bands played, and the lion dance was performed. A cloth-and-paper dragon carried by as many as a dozen young men wound its way along the streets, rolling its eyes and working its giant jaws. In 1930 the *Statesman* said: "The dragon and tiger that once made their way along the streets have not made an appearance for more than 10 years."[18] The author, as a child in 1930, experienced the Chinese dragon in a Portland New Year's parade and remembers it vividly. "The Passing of the Dragon" from Boise's parades would be regretted by those for whom it had been a colorful part of the city's life.

Other Chinese religious holidays are described in the chapter on Chinese Freemasons. See page 97.

III

Temples

廟

This drawing of Chinese worshipers in a Portland temple was published in *West Shore* magazine in 1889. It suggests what a similar occasion in Boise might have looked like.
ISHS SG 26/39

Soon after the first Chinese arrived in Boise, they set up a temple in one of the small wooden buildings on Idaho Street that made up the city's first Chinatown. An early resident remembered it as "a tiny lean-to."[1] Such places of worship were always called "Joss Houses" by the white community.

["Joss" is Pidgin English for God, from the Portuguese "Deus." Pidgin is a trade jargon used on the south China coast in the 19th century, and still used in New Guinea and some Pacific islands. It was the standard form of communication between whites and Chinese in Boise's Chinatown. Newspaper stories about the Chinese often used Pidgin words like "Melican" for American, "chop chop" for quickly, "savvy" for understand, "look see" for look, "can do" for can, "chow chow" for food,

This illustration from the same issue of *West Shore* shows banners from a temple in Portland being paraded, much as similar ones would be in Boise many years later.
ISHS SG 26.40

PROCESSION of PRIESTS
AND WORSHIPERS

Boise Chinese on parade in 1911 bear a close resemblance to the Portland paraders of 1889.
ISHS 26/21

etc.. These and other Pidgin words are part of American speech today, and some will be familiar to the reader.[2]]

The Chinese Masons were already building a three story-brick lodge hall on Front Street in 1901 that would have a temple on the top floor,[3] when the City Council condemned the Chinese wooden buildings on Idaho Street in September of that year. The room for the temple was 100 feet long, with an altar at one end. "The accessories of this altar are the most elaborate and expensive of any on the coast" said the *Statesman* in a 1917 article that included the first photograph taken inside the temple.[4] Some of the carvings in this photograph are in the Idaho Historical Museum's recreation of a Chinese place of worship. They were donated in 1971 by Boiseans who had stored them for many years. The museum's exhibit lacks much of what is shown in this

Temple banners of richly embroidered silk were displayed outside on stands before they were carried in a 1909 parade. *ISHS 60-52.385*

photograph but still gives credence to the photo caption's claim that one of the carvings cost $1000.

When forced to relocate to Front Street the Chinese built a new Joss House at the northeast corner of Seventh and Front Street. A photograph of its altar was printed with the same 1917 article. "The embroidered banners on each side of the altar are exquisite pieces of Chinese handiwork and cost several hundred dollars," said the writer. "The brass jardiniere holds the punk sticks which burn in front of the altar."[5]

This Chinese temple was the subject of several *Statesman* feature stories over the years, most of them short on facts and long on romance. Harold Rhodenbaugh wrote a description of his visit to the building in 1930, during which he interviewed Ah Fah Sook, "the genial keeper of the joss house." Ah Fah Sook asked the reporter: "You want know luck?" He then lit some "punk sticks" in front of the altar and called on the temple god Chin Law Guan "in a musical undertone. 'We

The original of this photograph of the temple in the Chinese Masonic Hall was lost in a fire. This coarse-screened newspaper photo at least gives us an idea of what it looked like. The arch at top with the golden sun was recovered and is in the Idaho Historical Museum.
ISHS SG 26/54

will wait a few moments,' he says. 'Chin Law Guan may be in China, and it takes 15 minutes for him to come here through the earth. He come, like radio, when called. Sometimes he man, walk around, see everything. Sometimes he fly, sail around in air. You ask, he tell everything. He honest. What you do? He tell.'"[6]

Since we have no photographs of Chin Law Guan, the god of Boise's temple, Rhodenbaugh's description is useful: "The figure of the god is of bronze and appears to be very old. Fah Sook says it is ageless. 'Thousands years old,' he says. 'Never born, never die, live always!'" Fah Sook also told the reporter that the figure [the god brings himself] was brought to Boise in 1863 by some of the first Chinese to arrive. Since none had arrived in the area at that date, it is possible that it came with the first arrivals or was sent over from China sometime in the

The Idaho Historical Museum's reconstruction of a Chinese temple was made possible with artifacts donated by generous Boiseans in 1971–72. The Chinese Masonic Hall arch spans the exhibit.
ISHS SG 26/55

1860s. Virtually everything in Chinese temples in the American West was imported and from the evidence we have, was made in or around Canton (Guangzhou).[7]

Rhodenbaugh's description continues: "The joss house is an unpretentious affair from the outside. A sign over the doorway in Chinese characters tells that Chin Law Guan, the god, resides inside. Lettered panels by the door 'sing a song of good,' explains Fah Sook.

"It is a shambles inside, with lamps laden with dust hanging from the ceiling, banners in red and gold lettering, cryptic signs, posters, gold paper flowers, pewter candlesticks and vases, and brass jardinieres almost filling the place. On his throne the joss barely has elbow space, and there is little room for those who would learn their fortunes to kneel and touch the floor three times with their heads."[8]

The best illustrations we have of Chinese religious observances come from an 1889 article in *West Shore*, a

The magnificent carved representation of a Chinese classical opera in the museum's temple recreation is overlaid with gold leaf in two tones. It was made near Canton (Guangzhou) in 1885. The action depicted is dramatic. Note the swordplay at left.
ISHS SG 26/61

Greta Parnell, whose father had leased the land on Front Street to the Chinese in 1902, was given many priceless works of art when the Chinese moved away in the 1930s and '40s. This interior view of her apartment near the corner of Front and Capitol shows the opera carving now in the museum.
ISHS 72-28.15

magazine published in Portland, Oregon. Although the temple illustrated was much larger than Boise's little home of Chin Law Guan, since it was located in a much larger Chinatown, many of its features were very similar. Other illustrations by the talented artist who did these appear in other chapters of this book.[9]

On March 17, 1937, Eva Hunt Dockery, wrote in the *Idaho Statesman*:

> The last vestige of the glory that was once Boise's "Chinatown" has gone. With the demolition of the joss house at the corner of Seventh and Front streets Tuesday, the last building used for ceremonial purposes by the early Chinese settlers in Boise has disappeared.
>
> The crude building, which showed no hint of its interior picturesqueness, was built for the religious ceremonies of the early Chinese about 36 years ago . . . . The new building was an extremely plain affair with a "Joss," the altar with its rich pewter urn for holding the incense sticks, the ornate pewter vases for holding the artificial bouquets, and the tall pewter candlesticks holding decorated candles. On the altar was an ever-burning light, a wick floating in oil in a brass cage.
>
> Around the sides of the room were the gorgeous silken banners and circular tents, resting on red-wood standards, which were used in parades during the New Year's season. In front of the altar were bamboo mats on which the worshipers kneeled.
>
> In the rear of the building were the living quarters of the several priests whose duty it was to keep the eternal light burning and to perform such ceremonies as were required on special calendar days, and for funerals, weddings, and christenings.[10]

Eva Hunt Dockery was editor of the *Statesman's* Pioneer Page for many years, with an avid interest in local history. She came to Boise with her husband in 1898 and knew the Idaho Street Chinatown before its move to Front Street in 1901. Her writing, unlike that of

凝瑞氣

other writers about the Chinese, was accurate and sensitive. Mrs. Dockery died in December 1937, only a few months after writing the story quoted above.[11]

Other Chinese places of worship, although not called Joss Houses, were in the meeting places of the Hip Sing Tong and Hop Sing Tong, and one moved in 1926 from the Chinese Masonic Hall on Idaho Street to 612 Idaho Street, where it shared space with the Chinese Nationalist Party. The altar in the Hip Sing Tong Building was still used for worship by an elderly man living in the building just before its demolition in 1972.[12] That altar was moved to the Idaho Historical Museum and installed in the recreated Chinese temple there. The iron balcony from the Hip Sing Building was installed in front of this exhibit. It appears in some of the photographs shown here.

The god described in Harold Rhodenbaugh's article may have looked like this one from a California temple.
Arthur A. Hart photo

IV

Christians

基督教

These Chinese men were members of an Americanization class sponsored by Boise's First Methodist Episcopal Church in 1904. They received instruction in the English language and in Christian religion. Later church classes in Americanization included whole families.
ISHS 72-56.4

Adding Christian beliefs to their own traditional ones was not difficult for some Chinese who were reached by Jesuit missionaries in the early 17th century or by Protestants in the early 19th century. Most Chinese resisted all western culture, however, considering it part of an imperialism that tried to force its commerce, values, and customs on their own. In the Chinese mind their ancient culture was far superior, and all westerners were barbarians.[1] This was powerfully expressed by the people of Canton in 1842 in a statement agreed upon at a great public meeting: "Behold the vile English nation! Its people are at one time vultures, and then they are like wild beasts . . . (with) natures more greedy than anacondas or swine."[2] This expression of outrage was precipitated by the first Opium War described in a later chapter. The perceptions expressed were reinforced repeatedly over the next century by the actions of foreign powers that tried to "westernize" China and that seized control of its seaports and trading areas.

Chinese sojourners in the American West proved themselves to be models of patience and forbearance in the face of intolerance and persecution by people who were at least nominally Christian. The Chinese in Idaho could teach Christians a lot about "turning the other cheek." That the Chinese fully understood the implications of this anomaly was revealed tellingly in an 1876 incident reported in the *Statesman.* When a Chinese man was pushed violently off the sidewalk into the street by a young hoodlum, he sharply remarked: "I heathen; *you* Christian; goo'by."[3]

In 1869 Kum Lum, an "Americanized" Chinese in Boise, received a letter from a San Francisco missionary asking him to undertake the work of spreading the gospel to his Chinese neighbors in Idaho by distributing books and tracts. Kum Lum, who had embraced Christianity several years earlier and who could read, write, and speak English fluently, accepted the responsibility.[4] In 1872, "Rev. George Kum Lum" returned to Boise under the auspices of the American Home Missionary Society to begin "preaching the true religion to his celestial brethren."[5] Within a few years Chinese converts were being ordained as ministers in several Christian denominations throughout the western states.[6] Boise's Episcopalians opened a Chinese Mission School, as did the Methodists.[7] The Presbyterians and others received Chinese families into membership. Of the present descendants of the city's pioneer Chinese families about half are Christian, but in most cases also observe traditional Chinese religious rituals as well, especially at New Years or festivals honoring dead ancestors.[8]

Louie Quong and his family were prominent members of Boise's First Presbyterian Church. One of the grandfathers had been a lay worker in a Presbyterian mission in China. When Mrs. Quong died in 1923 leaving small children, church members rallied to help Quong keep his family together. He hired a housekeeper to care for them, and in 1926 married a young woman recently arrived from Hong Kong. Mabel Quong was a devout Christian who raised her children in the faith. She proved to be a dedicated mother, hard worker, and shrewd businesswoman. It was she who started what would become the largest strawberry farm in Boise Valley near Eagle.

In 1927 Quong sent 17-year-old May, the oldest daughter by his first wife, to Canton to visit relatives and to learn the language and culture of China. She told the *Statesman* she was interested in "The Younger China" and the Nationalist movement. As a junior at Boise High School, May had been active in the Y.W.C.A. and the Girl Reserves.[9]

When the Quongs lost their home to a Christmas Eve fire in 1931, fellow Presbyterians offered to take them in until they could get resettled. At that time Louie retired from his farm in what is now Garden City to take his family to China, intending to settle there permanently. In 1932 Mabel adopted teen-age Chow Lun Wong in Hong Kong and enrolled her in a private girls' school, but after only a year the Quongs decided to return to Boise and to farming, this time near Eagle.

In 1937 Mabel arranged a marriage between her adopted daughter in China and Boise herbalist Yick Yee. They met for the first time in Los Angeles where a Chinese Christian minister performed the wedding ceremony. Chow Lun Wong adopted the name Faye after she came to Boise as Mrs. Yick Yee. Like Mabel Quong, who had helped her come to America, Faye was also a devout Christian and raised her six children as Christian also.

The Yees still celebrate the Chinese New Year festival, and sometimes the Fourth of July, with Boise's Fongs and Quongs who trace their origins to the same group of small villages in Guangdong.[10]

新年

NEW YEAR

V

Laundrymen

洗衣館

One of the first jobs taken up by Chinese immigrants in the American West was washing and ironing clothes for whites. A Chinese laundryman named Hop Kee was killed in Idaho City in September of 1865 by "a worthless scapegoat named Kurtz."[1] Herman Kurtz was tried and convicted of murder in the first degree and sentenced to hang, but territorial governor Caleb Lyon commuted his sentence to life imprisonment. The *Idaho World* reported: "Hitherto they [the Chinese] have been contented with 'washee close (sic) John . . ." but that they had begun mining on Mores Creek for the first time.[2] By 1870 there would be more Chinese miners than white miners in Idaho, with 1,754 of them in Boise County alone. Ada County had only 78, of which 65 were in Boise City.[3]

Chinese laundries made the news regularly in Boise in the 1870s because of the occurrence of fires in their wash houses. An 1875 incident led the paper to say "it is sure as fate, that unless some precaution is taken against the recklessness of these celestial cusses, who have fires, while ironing, all hours of the night, they will burn that portion of the city."[4] Of course the very nature of their work required the laundrymen to keep their wood stoves going. They needed to heat water for washing clothes, to keep irons hot for pressing them; by 1881, the Chinese were reportedly paying $120 to $150 a year for firewood.[5] All laundry was done the hard way in the 19th century, and the Chinese laundrymen relieved Boise housewives who could afford it of one of their most onerous tasks. No matter if the temperature outside was 100 degrees, wash-day fires in the kitchen had to be kept going.

When a Chinese laundryman died in January of 1877, the *Statesman* reported that his countrymen claimed to have seen his ghost every night in his old washhouse. "He walks up and down the house all night, slams doors, and occasionally sits down upon the body of any live heathen who happens to be sleeping in the room. Sam is probably after some of the many bills due him."[6]

All of the Chinese washhouses on Idaho Street had

Most Idaho towns had Chinese laundries in the 19th century. This group in Delamar, an Owyhee County mining community, is listening to a countryman play a three-stringed guitar. The ramshackle buildings they occupied were much like those on Idaho Street in Boise's early Chinatown.
ISHS 83-37.22

a problem disposing of waste-water. Their attempts to dig drain channels to the ditch that powered Cyrus Jacobs's mill were in part responsible for the later Chinese tunnel myth that persists to this day. The *Statesman* considered this drainage system a health hazard in the 1880s, at a time when strong anti-Chinese sentiment was running high. An 1881 *Statesman* story encouraged the opening of a white laundry at the Warm Springs east of the city because the "Chinese are taking too much money back to 'the Flowery Kingdom.'"[7]

At least a few were able to go home with wealth to show for lives of hard work and thrift. According to an 1892 report, "Sing High, a well known Chinese laundryman, left Boise yesterday on his way to China. He took with him $14,000 in money, the result of many years labor in Idaho."[8] For him, at least, the dream of every Chinese who came to America was realized.

The City Council passed an ordinance in 1886 creating a fire district in the center of the city requiring all new construction thereafter to be of brick or stone; laun-

This brass atomizer was used by Boise laundrymen for spraying clothes with water while ironing. Before using this kind of device the Chinese had simply sprayed water from their mouths—a practice that caused them to be slandered by white laundries that called it "spitting on your clothes."
ISHS collection

dries were banned altogether. This ordinance was not enforced until August of 1893, when all Chinese laundrymen within the district were arrested. They pleaded guilty and were given until October to relocate.[9] The deadline for the move was extended later until September 1, 1894.[10] By that time laundries within the district had moved into space in brick buildings rented from white owners.

The fire danger in Chinese laundries was always great, and not just in Boise. In 1901 two Nampa laundrymen died when their building burned. "A very large amount of money was in the building" reported the *Statesman.*[11] In Payette that same year, citizens petitioned the council to move Chinese laundries out of town.[12]

Despite earlier ordinances and their various amendments, a new Chinese laundry opened on Main Street between Tenth and Eleventh streets in 1901. The council received a complaint about it and the city attorney was instructed to draft a new ordinance prohibiting Chinese laundries on Main Street.[13] That no such ordinance was ever passed, was no doubt because people had come to rely on the Chinese for this work and wanted laundries in convenient locations. In almost all cases the buildings were owned by Caucasians and rented to the Chinese, and they conformed to the fire code by being built of brick.[14]

In the years between 1905 and 1911 five Chinese laundries operated in Boise.[15] In 1906 half of Boise's laundries were still Chinese, and all of them were located within the fire district—one on Main Street, two on Idaho, one on South Ninth, and one on South Tenth. There were two white laundries on Main as well.[16]

Quong Sing was located at 1014 West Idaho for many years, and Sing Lee at 506 Main. Phonetic spelling of Chinese surnames varied so widely that it is possible that the Chung Sin who operated a laundry at 617 West Idaho in 1925 is the same man listed as Quong Sing in 1905. His ad in Polk's 1921 city directory read: "All Hand Work, We Save Your Clothes. Satisfaction Guaranteed."[17] By 1925 only two Chinese laundries were left, Chung Sing and Quong Chong at 1013 Bannock.[18] The *Statesman* attributed the passing of the Chinese laundries to the facts that most homes in Boise now had electric washing machines and that gardening and restaurants had become more profitable businesses for Chinese.[19]

The Ching Sing laundry at 617 Idaho Street was still operating in 1935—the last listed in city directories.[20] This may or may not be yet another spelling of Quong Sing, Chung Sin, or Chung Sing; in any case the address remained the same for what was clearly a successful Chinese laundry business for more than half a century.

VI

Gardeners

菜園

This fine drawing of Chinese gardeners starting off on their early morning delivery routes was published in Portland's *West Shore* magazine in 1889. The scene could just as well have been drawn by the artist in Chinese gardens along Boise River.
ISHS SG 27/4

This *West Shore* drawing of a Portland vegetable man fits the description of a service available to Boise housewives from the 1870s until the 1920s.
ISHS SG 27/13

A photograph labeled only "Chinese gardener and vegetable man," shows his preference for traditional clothing and his pride in displaying a gold watch and chain. He wears his queue wrapped around his head, as was typical before the fall of the Qing Dynasty in 1911 when most Chinese men had theirs cut off to show their support of the new Republic of China.
ISHS 72-56.3

"The China population are planting gardens here pretty extensively. They are so patient and puttering that they do well," reported the *Idaho Tri-weekly Statesman* in April, 1871.[1] The Chinese who came to Idaho in the gold-rush days had not been miners at home. They were peasant farmers from small villages in the fertile deltas of Guangdong province. When mining or other

This gardener for a well-to-do Boise family wore American clothing.
ISHS collection

employment ran out in their new country, they turned to what they knew best, and at which they were highly skilled.

Chinese gardens flourished in Boise valley for the next century, supplying households, grocery stores, and restaurants with fresh produce daily. The *Statesman* noted on July 20, 1871, that the gardener "makes his appearance at our doors bright and early every morning, with the traditional pole and baskets, the latter filled with every variety of fresh plucked and cool vegetables."[2] People still living in Boise recall Chinese gardeners delivering produce to their homes in the 1920s and '30s in

Louie Do Gee was one of the pioneer gardeners who raised vegetables in what is now Garden City. This Walter Lubkin photograph from 1926 shows him beside his delivery truck in a Boise residential neighborhood. *ISHS 76-114.6*

Model T Ford trucks. Before they got trucks they used horse-drawn wagons. Boise's Louie family, in Idaho since the 1860s, were in the business until the 1970s, and the Quong family until the 1990s.[3]

That the Chinese were masters of the art of gardening was attested to frequently in the press, as in the *Idaho World* of Idaho City in May, 1869. "The industrious gardener has brought the ground to a high condition of culture, and from the small plat he yearly earns a sum that would be a fortune in itself to one of his own class in his native land. [They] have certainly the art of raising a greater variety and amount of vegetables from a small plat of ground than our own people have yet learned to do."[4]

The hard-working, inoffensive Chinese had more to worry about than growing fine crops. In December of 1890 Mayor James A. Pinney told the City Council, "The Chinese gardeners near the river are suffering

Bicycles were all the rage in the 1890s when this unidentified Boise Chinese man took his well-equipped machine to the photographer's studio to have his portrait made.
ISHS 72-56.2

many indignities at the hands of hoodlums and other roughs who break down the fences, and stone the Chinamen, and in other ways seek to injure these peaceable and well disposed individuals. They are entitled to the protection of the law and the officers should make efforts to arrest those who molest them."[5] Some of Boise's wealthy Chinese merchants offered a $25 reward that year for every conviction of those responsible for the outrages.[6]

The much-abused Chinese sometimes fought back by shooting at nocturnal visitors who stole their watermelons and other produce. The paper reported that gunfire punctuated the silence at night along the river.[7] Some of these thieves were boys who no doubt thought of their raids on the gardens as pranks; luckily for them none

William Louie carried on his father's Louie Gee Garden in Boise while his family was still in China. This envelope, with the logo of the garden, was on a letter sent to them on December 26, 1934.
Courtesy Andy Louie

were shot but it may have scared them away. On one occasion a cow was hit by mistake and had to be paid for by the Chinese gardener.[8]

At the turn of the century Chinese farmers in Boise Valley were producing large enough crops that they could ship them to other markets by rail. In May, 1902, they were sending produce to Montana towns nearly every day.[9]

When America entered the first World War in April of 1917, Boiseans were urged to join in a government program to plant gardens in vacant lots around the city to help in the war effort, much as Victory Gardens would be encouraged in World War II. The Chinese gardeners feared that this would ruin their livelihood since their spring vegetables were already planted and starting to come up. It was too late to switch to other crops. J.K. White, State Pure Food Commissioner in charge of the program, received an angry delegation asking him to stop the campaign. "You talk too much [about growing vegetables]" the spokesman told the commissioner.[10]

Chinese farm families who decided to try another business often opened restaurants where new arrivals in

William Louie, son of Louie Do Gee, one of the proprietors of the Louie Gee Garden.
Courtesy Andy Louie

Boise's Chinatown could usually find work as dishwashers or waiters. This was especially true if a kinship existed with the proprietor through their having come from the same village in Guangdong. They might also be connected through the Hip Sing or Hop Sing tong or a family association like the Soo Yuen tong made up of Louies, Fongs, and Kwongs. When a new business failed, as many did during the Great Depression of the 1930s, Chinese families then returned to farming where they could at least produce their own food, and perhaps enough extra to sell. Typically, like white farmers of that time, they grew fruits and vegetables, kept a cow for milk, butter, and cheese, raised poultry for eggs and meat, and had a work horse or two.[11]

Boise's Louie family history illustrates well the pat-

Little Andy Louie is held by grandfather Louie Do Gee in the ancestral village of Fok Sing in Guangdong province in this 1933 photo. His cousin May is the little girl in the foreground.
Courtesy Andy Louie

Andy Louie, right, returned to the family gardens near Strawberry Glen after service in the army during the Korean War. He would go on to a degree in pharmacy from Idaho State University. His young cousin Arthur, at left, is now a cardiologist in San Jose, California. They were harvesting onions when this 1961 snapshot was made.
Courtesy Andy Louie

tern of the return to farming when other businesses did not turn out well. Louie Ah Su was the first sojourner of his family from Tai Shan in the Pearl River delta to arrive in Idaho. He was a miner in Boise Basin in the late 19th century before he came to Boise and started a small garden in the north end. By then the population of towns like Idaho City and Placerville had dwindled and most of the Chinese had already left. When Ah Su returned to China, he sent his son Do Gee to Idaho to take over the gardens in Boise. Louie Do Gee leased land along the Boise River in what is now Garden City. His sons William and Tong came to Idaho from China in the early 1920s and successfully operated the Louie Gee Gardens until 1946, when the incorporation of Garden City forced them to give up the land they had leased from the Davis family, descendants of Tom and Julia Davis.[12]

A history of Idaho published in 1920 describes the Davis property as follows:

> The Thomas J. Davis Estate . . . embraces large realty interests . . . including about seven hundred acres of fine lands in the Boise valley along the river just west of the city—lands that are most fertile and productive and which include the beautiful and famous Chinese gardens, visible to and admired by all travelers on the Nampa Interurban Railway line, which follows the crest of the hill above the gardens . . . . These Chinese gardens are all on the Thomas J. Davis estate and constitute one of the most beautiful sights in the valley of Boise through the summer seasons.[13]

Do Gee returned to China a few years after the above was written, and he died there in 1942. Son Tong remained in Boise and operated the popular Shang Hai Low Restaurant on Capitol Boulevard until his death in 1951. Son William returned to the area that year from California, after two business ventures failed. He and his son-in-law Philip Lee reopened the Louie Gee Gardens on 30 acres of land west of Garden City at Strawberry Glen. This business prospered, with all of the children working hard as they grew up.

William's son Andy came over from China in 1949, first to California and then to Boise Valley with the family. He went into the service during the Korean War and was stationed in an army hospital in Germany for two years. He would eventually earn a degree in Pharmacy from Idaho State University and do graduate work in administration at the University of Colorado. He retired in 1997 from his position as administrator at Holy Rosary Hospital in Ontario, Oregon. The Louie Gee Gardens closed in 1964 when William Louie retired, and Philip Lee went back to California to operate a successful supermarket.[14]

Andy Louie's generation of Chinese-Americans were typically college graduates, often with advanced degrees in the professions of medicine, law, and administration. None of them farm any more, and the Chinese gardens have faded into history. The names Garden City and its main thoroughfare Chinden Boulevard (a contraction of Chinese garden), remain as memorials to those pioneer farmers.

VII

Cooks and Cooking

This man cooked for a Boise family and was a general house servant. He and others in such domestic positions also took care of the family's small children.
ISHS collection

Leona Hailey Cartee, writing to an Eastern friend who had asked about the hardships pioneer women in the West had to endure, said: "As I think of those dear women in the early Seventies it seems to me they were happy and life was not so hard. Money was plentiful, nearly everyone that I knew had a Chinese cook, and usually he was not only the cook but general house boy—washing, ironing and doing all the heavy work."[1]

The 1870 census for Boise City confirms that what she recalled was true –at least for families like hers that were well off. Thirteen Chinese men whose occupation was reported were listed as cooks. Jim Waea, 21, who worked for the Haileys was reported as a "house servant", performing the tasks Leona had described.

Edward J. Curtis, Territorial Secretary, had a 20

Chinese cooks found employment on farms and ranches in Boise Valley, and others cooked for hotels, restaurants, and boarding houses.
ISHS collection

year-old-cook named Sam Sing, and prosperous brewer John Lemp had a cook recorded as "Ai Schin". One suspects that the "Sch" prefix was this German family's phonetic spelling of a name usually rendered "Shin," The Lemps had 13 children and certainly needed domestic help. Six other Chinese cooks worked in private homes, and three worked in hotels. Two more cooked for a boarding house. The oldest was 35, the youngest, Long Tan, only 16.[2] Where, we wonder, did these young men learn to cook?

The *Statesman* editorialized in August, 1876, against paying the Chinese cooks too much. "It has been the custom, with some people here, when they find their neighbor has a good Chinese cook, to offer the Mongolian a dollar or two extra wages per week, and

BOISE CITY DIRECTORY. 85

CHINA TOM & CO, Restaurant, 704 W Main, Bell Tel 236-A.
(See adv.)

CHINA TOM & CO.

704 W. MAIN ST

FIRST CLASS IN EVERY RESPECT.
DINING ROOM FOR LADIES.

BOISE, IDAHO.

Chinese Cemetery, Morris Hill, 2 miles s w of city.
Chinese Joss House, Front n e cor 7th.

-426 DOOLY BLDG. SALT LAKE CITY, P. O. BOX

. Forrester. C

China Tom & Co. ran a popular Main Street restaurant from 1901 until 1907. This is his ad in the 1905 city directory.
Idaho Historical Library

thus get him. This is neither right nor honorable, and it spoils the Chinamen . . . they have been petted and coaxed until they are completely spoiled." The paper suggested that five dollars a week would be "big wages for the best of them."[3]

At the height of anti-Chinese sentiment in 1885, the proprietor of the United States Restaurant advertised "all white labor" and called attention to the fact by offering a $100 reward to anyone who could find a Chinese anywhere on the premises.[4] Ironically, the United States Restaurant would later be taken over by Chinese owners who ran it successfully for several years.[5]

James Griffin, proprietor of the Overland House—the city's leading hotel since the 1860s—employed Chinese cooks, as did the Eastman Brothers who bought it and operated it until 1905. E.W. Johnson, manager of the hotel in 1903, fired his Chinese cooks that year and secured "a full crew of first class white help from Salt Lake City."[6]

The Chinese began to open their own restaurants in the 1890s. This elicited an ad from a white restaurant owner that read: "Go to the Anti-Chinese Restaurant for first-class boarding. A cigar given with every meal."[7] In 1892 the *Statesman* reported: "Another Chinese Restaurant is being fitted up on the north side of Main

Louie Lai's Chong Wah Low Restaurant featured noodles and chop suey. It operated at 105 North Seventh Street from 1918 until 1931.
ISHS

Street between Sixth and Seventh streets. There are already three Chinese eating houses and one Chinese laundry in the block, and with the fifth establishment about ready for business the pigtails may be said to have fairly captured the neighborhood."[8]

The new restaurant, owned by Pon Sing, advertised regularly in the newspaper. His Pacific Chop House featured American menus, specializing in "fresh eggs, steaks, chops, oysters and a splendid variety of well cooked food." Lake Yuen was mentioned as "in charge of the culinary department." Board at this restaurant, which stayed open all night, was $4.50 per week.[9]

In December, 1893, Jim & Co. announced the grand opening of the Bon Ton Chop House, formerly the Silver City Chop House. The menu published for the grand

The Chong Wah Low was decorated with lanterns and carvings imported from China. Proprietor Louie Lai is at right.
ISHS

opening was impressive: soup, boiled salmon with egg sauce, a choice of turkey with cranberry sauce, young chicken with dressing and gravy, sirloin of beef, loin of pork, or loin of veal, and a choice of lemon meringue or apple pie. The cost, in that depression year, was 25 cents.[10]

What most Americans regard as traditional Cantonese food was invented in this country and unknown in China. Chop suey, for example, made its debut in 1896 during the visit to America of the great Chinese diplomat Li Hung Chang. Tradition says that chefs he brought with him created the dish for a banquet Li hosted for American guests in New York City. This representative of the Emperor of China created quite a stir wherever he went. His visit was widely covered in American newspapers, and public interest in everything Chinese soared. According to the Library of Congress "After 1896 Americans began to visit Chinese restaurants in large numbers for the first time. A chop suey fad swept big cities such as New York and San Francisco."[11]

Harry Fong, right, seen here with a business associate, was the acknowledged leader of Chinatown in the 1930s, in part because he was thoroughly Americanized and could serve as a go-between with city officials. He was one of the few Chinese businessmen in Boise fluent in English.
ISHS

In the 1890s Boise's Chinese restaurants served only standard American food like that mentioned in Jim & Co.'s ad of 1893. That they also served liquor at that time is revealed by the fact that owners Fong Lee, Sang Woo, Quan Chong, Fook Ching Tong Duck Woo, and Bon Hong were summoned to police court for not having city liquor licenses, although they did have federal retail licenses.[12] Chinese were still not welcome elsewhere in Idaho. Charlie Tong, who had opened a restaurant in Emmett, was chased out of town in February, 1903, along with another Chinese and a Japanese employed there.[13] The new town of Twin Falls reacted in similar bigoted fashion in 1904 when a large crowd escorted a Chinese chef from the town by torchlight after he was hired by a local restaurant. The paper proudly reported that the act was accompanied with "no threats or even the thought of violence."[14]

Harry Fong started his Boise career in 1923 as a cook in the Sunshine Café. He later owned and operated the Bamboo Garden on Capitol Boulevard.
ISHS 71-156.6

Boise's Chinese restaurants continued to flourish in the early 20th century. Some were in the New Chinatown that had moved to Front Street, but most still operated on Main Street. China Tom & Co. was in three different Main Street locations between 1901 and 1907. Fong & Co. had two restaurants on Main called The State and The U.S. from 1905 until 1911.[15] Boiseans had become fond of Chinese food by then. Menus included noodles, chop suey, chow mein, sweet and sour pork, and rice. In 1908 the "Household Hints Department" of the *Idaho Statesman* offered prizes for Chinese cookery. "Natives of the Flowery Kingdom are especially invited

In 1927 Harry Fong went to China and brought back an 18-year-old bride who had never before been out of the small peasant village in Guangdong where she was born. She was welcomed warmly by the community as "the first lady of Chinatown." She took the name Gretta, and helped her husband run the Bamboo Garden Restaurant.
ISHS 71-156.11

to contribute. Those dishes most attractive to the American taste and most practical in the Occidental kitchen will be given first honors." First prize was three dollars; the next three collected one dollar each.[16]

In 1909 the Shang Hai Low began a long run as one of the city's popular eating places. Its competitors in that era were Lam Lin Ark's Palace Café, the Man Far Low, and the Peking Restaurant on Idaho Street. Chinatown was now firmly established around the intersection of Front and 7th streets (now Capitol Boulevard) but Main Street still had two Chinese restaurants.[17]

The christening of the new baby son of Mr. and Mrs. Fong Yow in September of 1924 was an occasion for a grand feast, to which 30 prominent citizens and public officials were invited. At four tables set up in the Shang

Harry and Gretta Fong with their firstborn son Harry, Jr. This baby died in infancy. They had three more children before Gretta's death in 1937.
ISHS 71-156.8

Hai Low, guests were served birds' nest soup, chicken with pineapple, fried spareribs with pineapple and bamboo sprouts, chicken and bamboo omelet, duck with mushrooms and chestnuts, and several other entrees. American ice cream and sunshine cake were served as dessert. "During the repast, the host, Fong Yow, made a little speech of welcome in which he expressed his pleasure in having his American friends with him, and his firm belief in upholding the government and its laws." The assurance was given at a time when clashes between the Hip Sing and On Leong tongs were creating headlines in Chinatowns across the country. Boise's Chinese hoped to isolate themselves from these clashes, but were not always able to do so.[18] (Boise has never had an On Leong tong).

Young Albert Louie, at right in this studio picture made in China, would come to Boise and become the proprietor of the House of Louie Restaurant on Capitol Boulevard near Main. Joanne Louie, holding baby May, was the wife of Tong Louie, one of the partners in the Louie Gee Garden.
Courtesy Andy Louie

Fong Yow and his wife named their baby boy Eugene Sherman Yow after Boise's mayor, who was present with Mrs. Sherman. The Fong Yows named another of their sons for Dr. George Collister, whose name is prominent in Boise history. The guest list included Senator William E. Borah, federal Judge F.S. Dietrich, Mrs. C.C. Moore (her husband, the governor, was out of town), and prominent businessmen.. Following these festivities a second banquet was served for 30 Chinese guests.[19]

Fong Lou, who according to the *Statesman* had lived in Boise for 20 years as a partner in the Shang Hai

Low,[20] opened his own Hong Kong Café on Idaho Street in May of 1926.

Chinese feasts to which local officials were invited were regular events in the Twenties. In 1927 the Shang Hai Low was the scene of a party for 80 guests to introduce the new bride of Harry Fong, who had just arrived from China. The mayor, the chief of police, and other prominent Boiseans were present. Fong had earlier introduced his bride to 150 local Chinese with a similar banquet.[21] American guests were often invited to help celebrate Chinese New Years, and elaborate spreads were laid out in the Hop Sing Tong headquarters as well as in restaurants.

In the 1930s Harry and Gretta Fong ran the Bamboo Garden at 211 Capitol Boulevard. Henry Fong was a waiter there. Park Wing and Yow Fong were cooks at the Shang Hai Low. In 1940 the city had four Chinese restaurants: the Shang Hai Low, the Bamboo Garden, Joe Chin's at 202 South Capitol, and Fong's Tea Garden at 624 Idaho Street. By 1950 only three were left, the fewest Chinese restaurants in the city in 40 years.[22]

By the 1980s the Louie family dominated the local Chinese businesses. Albert and Jean ran the House of Louie on Capitol Boulevard; Larry and Shirley Louie had the popular Golden Star on Orchard Street, opened in 1965; Art and Alice Louie owned the Twin Dragon and the Golden Dragon. This prominent Chinese family has been in the city for more than a century.[23]

Today, as this is written in 2002, there are 18 Chinese restaurants in the area, several of them serving spicy Mandarin and Szechwan dishes in addition to traditional Cantonese favorites. There are also five Vietnamese restaurants and two specializing in Thai cuisine—a legacy of the Vietnam war era when many American servicemen developed a taste for Indo-Chinese food, and many refugees from Southeast Asia came to America. Wok cooking and Mongolian barbecue are attractions that have caught on in recent years, and "all you can eat" fixed-price buffets offer a choice of dozens of dishes.

醫藥

VIII

Doctors

C.K. Ah Fong was Idaho's most noted Chinese doctor. He was the first of his race to be licensed by the State of Idaho—a right he had to fight for in the courts.
ISHS 81-2.32

Moc Ping, Fong Wee, Lee Tin, Wing Lee, Wang Yang Sing, Gee Wa, Louie Bow, Tong Lee, and Chin Man Sui all practiced Chinese herbal medicine in Boise in the 19th and early 20th centuries, and enjoyed liberal patronage from the white community. But the Ah Fong family of doctors had the longest continuous practice in Boise, spanning more than a century.

C.K. Ah Fong, patriarch of the family in Idaho, was born in Canton on October 5, 1844, son of Dr. Whey Fong. After training with his father, first in China and then in San Francisco, C.K. came to Idaho in 1866. He settled in Atlanta and then spent some time in Rocky Bar before coming to Boise in 1889. C.K.'s father practiced herbal medicine in San Francisco before returning to China to spend his last years—as most of the first generation of sojourners in America hoped to do.[1]

C.K. Ah Fong advertised regularly in Boise newspapers and city directories, as did other Chinese doctors. His ad in the 1893 directory listed him as "Chinese

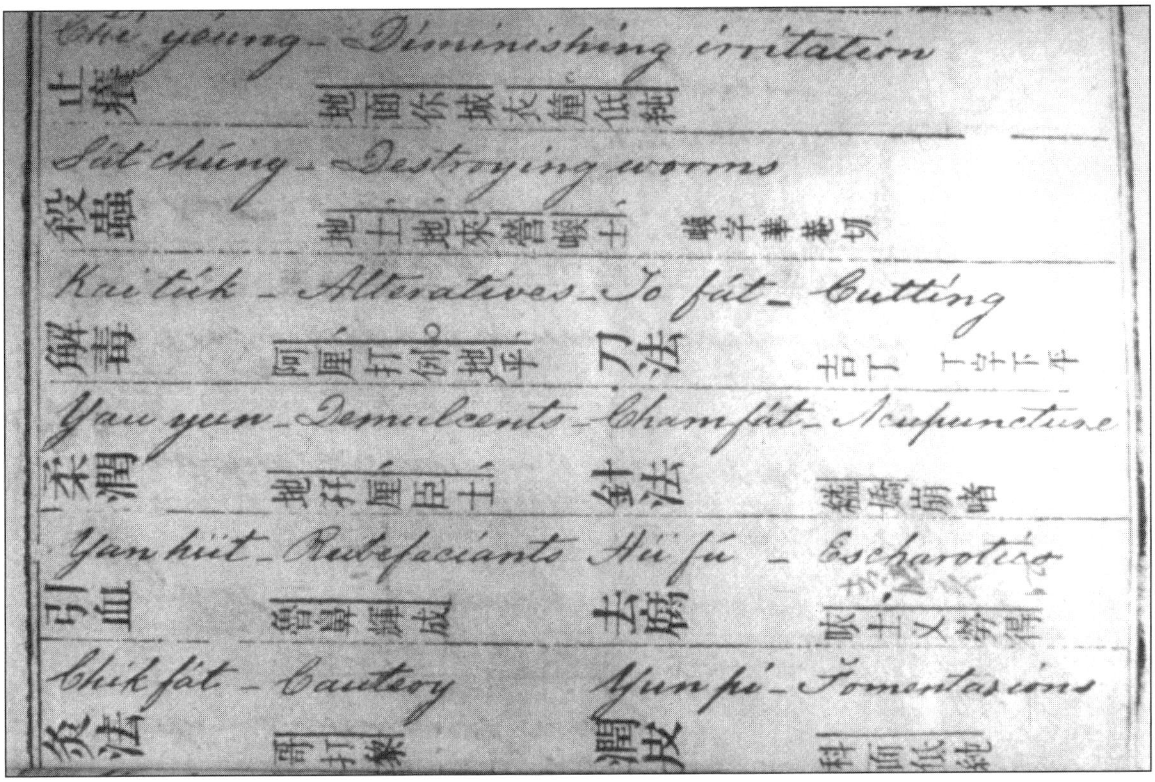

This detail of a book in C.K. Ah Fong's medical library shows a bilingual reference to acupuncture.
ISHS SG 26/95

Physician", and read: "All examinations conducted without questions. Disease located. Fevers and Rheumatic Pains cured. Also diseases of children a specialty, 12 years practice. 834 Idaho Street."[2] In 1904 his ad read: "Cure yourself by the use of Nature's remedies. Medicines direct from China."[3]

Three years later, Idaho was the only state or territory in the United States without a state medical society or board of examiners. Although the Territorial legislature passed an act in 1887 "to prevent the practice of medicine by unqualified persons," it had established no examining system.[4] Some feared that without such a board Idaho could become "a dumping ground for the poorly educated and the rejected applicants of other state's examining boards."[5] On September 12, 25 doctors from all parts of Idaho met in the council chambers of Boise's new city hall and formed a State Medical Society. The code of ethics of the American Medical Association was adopted and it was decided that only reputable grad-

AH FONG C K, Physician and Propr Ah Fong Herb Sanitarium, 210 N 7th, Bell Tel 10-F, res 614 W Idaho, Bell Tel 25-F, Ind 178. (See adv.)

DR. C. K. AH FONG,

HERB SANITARIUM.

210 N. Seventh Street, Boise, Idaho.

DISEASES OF MEN, WOMEN AND CHILDREN SUCCESSFULLY DIAGNOSED WITHOUT ASKING ANY QUESTIONS.

Cure Yourself by the use of Nature's Remedies. Medicines Direct from China. Forty Years' Successful Practice in Idaho.

AH FONG HERB SANITARIUM, Dr C K Ah Fong Propr, 210 N 7th, Bell Tel 10-F. (See adv.)

CHIN MAN SUI, Chinese Physician, 713 W Idaho, res same Bell Tel 420-B. (See adv.)

Dr. Chin Man Sui,

CHINESE HERB PHYSICIAN.

32 YEARS EXPERIENCE AND PRACTICE IN IDAHO.

713 W. IDAHO ST. BOISE, IDAHO.

FONG WEE, Chinese Druggist and Physician, 114 N 7th, res same, Bell Tel 781-A. (See adv.)

DR. FONG WEE,

Chinese Drugs and Medicines.
114 North Seventh Street.
Bell Telephone
781-A.

With ON WO HO & CO.,
7TH AND IDAHO STREETS. BOISE, IDAHO.

C.K. Ah Fong and other Boise Chinese doctors placed prominent notices of their practices in city directories. These are from 1905.
ISHS library collection

Gerald H. Ah Fong carried on the family traditional Chinese medical practice in the Hip Sing Building until the 1950s. This window is now in the Idaho Historical Museum's Chinese herb shop exhibit.
ISHS SG 26/46

uates of recognized medical colleges "of the regular school" be admitted to membership.[6] Clearly this excluded Chinese doctors.

At its second annual meeting, in 1894, the association announced that it would seek legislation to outlaw quackery "in all its moods, tenses, and declensions, dips, spurs, and angles.[7]

With the passage of a law establishing a medical licensing board, H.S. Wright, who had operated a drug store in Boise since the 1870s, was the first white practitioner arrested. Fong Lee and Chin Man Sui were the first Chinese.[8]

Chin was born in China in about 1847 and came to San Francisco in 1871, leaving behind a wife and son who never came to America. He had a practice in Whitebird, Idaho, and Sparta, Oregon, before coming to Boise in the early 1890s. According to his 1916 obituary, while in Whitebird he had shot and killed an Indian in self-defense.[9]

Chin Man Sui would continue to practice herbal medicine in Boise, despite frequent complaints by prominent members of the medical association that resulted in his being arrested and fined for practicing without a license. Dr. Chin was also arrested several more times

At the opening of the Idaho Historical Society's Chinese interiors in 1973, Dick Ah Fong played the part of his great-grandfather as he dispensed herbs to Vaughan Price, a volunteer from the Boise Little Theater.
ISHS photo

over the years for dispensing opium. His newspaper ads offered to treat all diseases of men and women by mail order: "Treatment sent to any address. Send for symptoms blank . . . Box 950." He also advertised, as many white medical practitioners did at the time, "Cancer cured or no charge."[10]

It would be interesting to know the reaction of Boise's Chinese herbalists to a full-page ad in the *Idaho Statesman* on Sunday, May 24, 1914, placed by San Francisco herbalist Lee K. Chin. It featured a large portrait of the doctor and the headline "Home Treatment Sent Free by Chinese Herbalist." A coupon listed 26 ailments that the reader could check and the statement "Send me at once, all charges paid, your Free Treatment for my case and your 64-page Medical Book—all entirely free to me." In another part of the ad Lee said, "I do not claim to cure cancer, leprosy or other really incurable diseases, but I do claim to cure, and actually and positively do cure, many diseases and complaints considered chronic and incurable . . . ."[11] Still active in Boise when this ad appeared were Fong Wee, who had been in Boise since 1904; Chin Man Sui; and C.K. Ah Fong, who had just returned from two years in China to visit old

San Francisco herbalist Lee K. Chin took a full page ad in the *Idaho Statesman* and other western newspapers to solicit mail order business. His portrait appeared with a lengthy description of traditional Chinese herbal medicine.
ISHS microfilm

friends and take a post-graduate course in traditional medicine.[12]

Although the ad might appear to be infringing on the practice of local herbalists, who also did a mail-order business, it probably helped them by explaining their ancient trade to the public. The Lee K. Chin page gave a long and detailed account of what herbal medicine was, its history, and the thorough training required to master it. "Do you know why Chinese physicians are obliged to study for ten to fifteen years, while European and American doctors can get off with three years in the university?" Chin asked. Then followed a list of some of the training required in China: A year of botany, growing and gathering herbs and learning the uses of 2000 plants, followed by two years of pulse diagnosis, "so that they acquire a marvelous knowledge of human ailments by this means."[13] (The technique is still being used in Boise today.)[14] When C.K. Ah Fong was refused a license by the state board of medical examiners in 1899, he filed suit in District Court that led to reversal of that decision. Judge George H. Stewart ordered the board to give Dr. Ah Fong a license.[15] His many white patients were no doubt grateful, for they had relied on his skills for many years. The esteem in which Dr. Ah Fong and his family were held by Boiseans was demonstrated in March, 1904, when his wife died at age 62. More than a thou-

The medical herbs are grown in great gardens

Plucked and dried under special conditions

Tending the carefully cultivated plants

Stripping bark and gathering tender leaves

These line drawings illustrated Lee K. Chin's account of how herbs were grown and harvested in China. Boise's herb doctors ordered their plant materials from the same Old Country sources.
ISHS microfilm

Yick and Faye Yee with their first child Virginia in front of their shop at 612 Idaho Street, 1939.
Courtesy Yee family

sand people attended the funeral services conducted by Congregational minister R.B. Wright. Hundreds, led by the Columbia Band, followed the cortege to Morris Hill cemetery. The *Idaho Statesman* said: "She was probably better and more favorably known to Idaho pioneers than any woman of her race in the state."[16]

The herbal medicine practiced by the Ah Fongs and other Chinese doctors in Boise is an ancient art developed in China over thousands of years. Lists of vegetable, animal, and mineral materials used for the treatment of specific ailments and diseases had been compiled from earliest times. The best known, still in use, is a *Materia Medica* from the Ming Dynasty (1368–1644 AD) that includes descriptions of 1,892 different medicines, and was undoubtedly a basic resource for Chinese doctors in Boise. The *Inner Cannon* (Nei Ching), an ancient compilation from more than two centuries B.C., is considered the theoretical framework of Chinese medicine, but descriptions of illnesses, medicines, and treatment have been dated from as far back as the Shang Dynasty (1766–1122 B.C.).[17] Medical books from the Ah Fong pharmacy, saved by the Idaho State Historical Society from the Hip Sing Association Building before its demo-

In 1943 Yick Yee sponsored a wartime salvage depot near his place of business. He is shown here with baby Grant, daughter Virginia, and wife Faye. Boise Chinese citizens contributed heavily to China's war against the Japanese by buying Chinese war bonds. After December 7, 1941, China and America were allies.
Courtesy Yee family

lition in 1972, refer to acupuncture as well as the uses of many medicines.

A large chest of drawers found in the building still contained roots, bark, dried leaves and berries from many plants, as well as dried horned lizards and other animal materials. Each drawer, prominently labeled in Chinese characters, can be seen today in The Idaho Historical Museum's Chinese exhibits. These materials were last used by Gerald Ah Fong, who dispensed herbal medicines in the Hip Sing Building until the 1960s, when the Communist takeover of mainland China made it impossible to import necessary herbs from there.[18]

Gerald Ah Fong was born in China in 1905, grandson of C.K. Ah Fong. He came to Boise and entered Lincoln School at age 11, unable to speak a word of English. After a difficult transition to a totally strange cul-

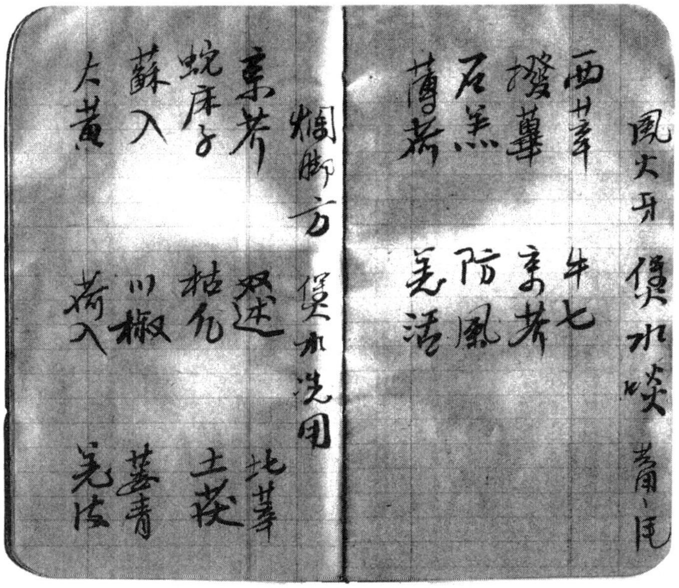

These pages from one of Yick Yee's prescription books display his graceful brushwork calligraphy. The one at left is for athlete's foot; on the right a gargle for inflammation of the gums.
Courtesy Yee family

ture, he learned so fast that the *Idaho Statesman* printed a feature headlined "Young Chinese Shows Ability in Many Lines." Gerald's athletic prowess, high grades, and artistic skills were praised. When given a book and a medal by the city's joint Americanization Committee in 1920, he asked that his aged grandfather, Dr. C.K. Ah Fong, be present to see him accept the prizes. "The proud old Oriental doctor occupied a seat upon the stage and beamed proudly on everyone."[19]

Herbert Ah Fong, Gerald's father, was also born in China. He shared a medical practice with his son at 611 Idaho Street before they moved to the Hip Sing Building on Seventh Street. Herbert never learned to speak more than broken English and returned to China when he retired. His grandson Dick Ah Fong recalls that the Communists extorted money from Gerald to keep the old man from harm.[20]

Yick Yee, a native of Canton, China, came to Boise from Tacoma in 1934 and opened the Goon Hoy Chinese Herb Company. He had arrived in San Francisco as a 16-year-old in 1909 and, like most immigrants who could speak no English, had to take whatever menial work he could get until he could return to China to learn the art of herbal medicine. He was advised to come to

Yick Yee moved his Goon Hoy herbal medicine shop to a former service station building at 6202 Fairview Avenue in the 1950s. He looks at us from a window decorated with flowers and Chinese porcelain figures.
Courtesy Yee family

Boise because herbalist Wing Lee had died in a plane crash on October 31, 1932, and two years later his stock in trade was still intact at 612 Idaho Street. Wing Lee, described as "one of the city's foremost flying enthusiasts" at the time of his death was performing acrobatics required to qualify for a pilot's license, when an aileron tore loose during a tailspin and he crashed on Fairview Avenue. His body was shipped to Hong Kong for burial where he was survived by a wife and a 10 year old son he had never seen.[21]

Yick Yee took over the Wing Lee business at 612 Idaho Street, where he paid a monthly rent of $18. "The first year was difficult for him, but he soon became well established because he could 'read' pulses . . . a skill that distinguished him from the other Chinese herbalists in Boise."[22] He also had the advantage of being able to speak English fluently and was often called upon to be an interpreter for the courts when Chinese got into trouble with the law. He sometimes put up bail for those he sympathized with, but he had no use for drug offenders.[23] Mortuary records indicate that on one occasion he paid funeral and burial expenses for an indigent Chinese, possibly because the man was a fellow member of the

Hop Sing Tong.[24] Yee was a lifelong member of that benevolent and protective organization, to which he contributed generously all his life. In his youth he had worked for the Tong as a gambler, but he didn't like it and decided there was no future in that line of work. When asked by his son years later why he had returned to China to study medicine, he said he wanted to obtain "something that fire could not burn, the wind could not blow away, the floods could not wash away nor the thieves steal." When his son asked what that was, he said, "knowledge."[25]

While studying in China, Yee married and had a son and daughter. In 1937, although his wife in China was still living, he married a second time. He had only seen Chow Lun Wong's photograph but went to Los Angeles to meet and marry her. Chow Lun Wong (Wai Oi), like so many Chinese brides in Boise's history, spoke no English and had to adjust to a totally foreign culture as fast as she could. From the beginning she worked hard to help support a family that grew to include six children, all of whom graduated from college, three with masters degrees and one with a doctorate.[26]

In an interview with Bob Lorimer of the *Idaho Statesman* in 1971, Yee admitted that he was very proud of his children and of what they had accomplished. The writer called it "a better-than-average American success story."[27] Yick Yee, last of the older generation of Chinese herbalists in Boise, died in January, 1973. He was 79. By then the family's friends included a governor of Idaho and two chief justices of the Idaho Supreme Court.[28]

In the years since Yick Yee and others retired or left Boise, a new generation of practitioners of Chinese traditional medicine has come to Boise. Acupuncture, virtually unknown in the western world until the 1950s, is one of the basic techniques used for the treatment of illnesses of all kinds, along with diagnostic pulse reading and herbal medication. In Chinese medicine health depends upon maintaining a balance between the Yin principal, negative and passive, and the Yang, positive and active. Keeping the flow of life energy in balance, along channels charted in ancient times, is assisted by the insertion of steel needles at more than 300 points along these channels. Acupuncture has proven especially effective for pain control.[29]

Of 15 acupuncturists listed in the yellow pages of the Boise telephone book in 2002, only three are Chinese and only two of those studied in China. The Occupational License Bureau of the State of Idaho began licensing acupuncturists in 1999. These practitioners are herbalists as well, combining all of the elements of traditional Chinese medicine in their work. Businesses that only dispense herbs are not licensed.[30]

The ancient healing arts of China, first brought to Idaho mining camps in the 1860s by C.K. Ah Fong and other pioneers, are available in Boise again, a reminder of one of the many roles played by the Chinese in Idaho history.

IX

Opium Dens

鴉片煙

When the Chinese came to Idaho in the 1860s, opium had been used in south China for centuries. Although the emperor had banned it, and even decreed a death penalty for its cultivation, sale, and use, enforcement was lax. Drug addiction worsened in the early 19th century when the British East India Company aggressively pushed the opium trade into Guangdong province, despite Chinese laws forbidding it. The exchange of Indian opium, derived from the Eurasian poppy *papaver somniferum*, for silver that was then used to buy tea and silk for the European Market, created a most favorable balance of trade for England and a disastrous one for China. Money was flowing out of the country at the same time that new masses of the population were becoming addicted.[1]

When Chinese officials confiscated and destroyed opium at the port of Canton, the British responded with attacks by naval and military forces. The Chinese were defeated in what have come to be known as the two Opium Wars, 1839–42 and 1858. The inability of the empire to resist foreign invasion of its ports and markets by European powers (and later by the United States and Japan) was revealed and exploited thereafter. The "foreign devils," as the Chinese called them, divided China into "spheres of influence" surrounding the principal seaports, forcing China to pay humiliating indemnities and to legalize the opium trade. Britain took possession of Hong Kong.[2]

Many Chinese who left their homes in the 1850s and '60s to seek economic opportunities in America and elsewhere throughout the world brought the opium habit with them. Its presence in Boise City's young Chinatown was noted in the *Idaho Tri-weekly Statesman's* 1871 comment on a recent fire: "As usual with ninety-nine-one-hundredths of fires of late in mountain cities this one originated in the China quarter . . . . Their lives are a debauch. They crowd together and drink and gamble all night, or steep their senses in the lethargy attendant on opium smoking, and these fires are the natural result."[3] The paper's own pages at the time suggest that aside from the use of opium, the debauchery of all-night drinking and gambling characterized the city's single white

Fan Tan was the favorite Chinese gambling game in early Boise. This 19th century photograph fits the written description of games in the city's Idaho Street Chinatown.
Courtesy Jan Lee, Sinotique, New York City

male population as well. Drunken fights, stabbings and shooting in saloons were regularly reported. The *Statesman* estimated that in the 1870s more than 100 murders had been committed in Idaho, with only five men brought to trial.[4] One of them, an Irish immigrant named Anthony McBride, was hanged at the mouth of Crane Creek on January 24, 1868, "for the wanton murder" of a Chinese. Nearly all of the violence reported at the time and throughout the 19th century was alcohol induced. Opium, on the other hand, for all its addictive power, made most of its users tranquil and non-violent.[5]

By 1879 the paper claimed that more than $7000 worth of the drug was smoked in Boise every year, and that "some white men and boys use a good deal of it." As sentiment built across Idaho and the West to drive out the Chinese, the *Statesman* was of the opinion that "breaking up the Chinese opium dens of this city ought to be gravely considered by our officials."[6]

In 1881 the Eleventh Session of the Idaho Territorial

Legislature passed a law "to prohibit the keeping of places of resort for smoking opium or frequenting same" and established penalties: a fine not to exceed $100 for operating a place where it was used or for being caught using it, and $50 for being found in such a place, whether using the drug or not. If one was unable to pay the fine, it could be worked off at the rate of one dollar per day for 10 hours at hard labor. Regular raids by Boise police followed this legislation and sequels to it for the next century. City ordinances followed, with amendments over the years—most often calling for increased penalties.[7] The *Statesman* noted on February 15, 1881, that "Marshals Robbins and Paxton have made several raids on the Chinese opium dens, without success."[8] However, these raids often resulted in the arrest of white addicts as well as Chinese. Typically, as in August of 1883, the smokers and keepers of dens were fined equally: $40 and costs. That year most served out their fines in jail at the rate of two dollars per day.[9] The opium pipes confiscated by police during these raids were often treasured heirlooms, and their loss was felt by owners more than the fines or incarceration. By the 1890s fines had increased, and convicted opium smokers were credited with only one dollar per day for jail time served.

Federal officers were sent to Boise in 1895 to raid opium dens and to seek out the source of the contraband that had been shipped into the city—estimated by one source at a thousand pounds a month. "This city seems to be a general supply point for this entire portion of the state," the *Idaho Statesman* commented.[10]

Workmen repairing Eighth Street between Main and Idaho in June, 1898, uncovered a large hole in front of the Odd Fellows Hall. It was the paper's opinion that it was an underground opium den from the city's early days when the area was part of Chinatown. A white man called "Chinese Anthony," because of his association with the Chinese, had owned the adjoining property.[11] This, and earlier incidents, as when a team of horses fell through rotting planks into a series of excavations behind Chinese buildings on Idaho Street in 1888, contributed to the legend repeated to this day, that the city is honeycombed with Chinese tunnels. In the latter case, the *Idaho Statesman* called the place "a regular sinkhole for sewerage."[12] Excavations dug off Chinese cellars, some used for opium smoking, but the only "tunnels" were primitive cesspools to collect both sewerage and the runoff from Chinese laundries. Many complaints were made of the smell of these sewer tunnels before the city completed the first phase of a municipal sewer system in February of 1892. It would be more than a year before constant threats of arrest and the levying of stiff fines would force some prominent white citizens to connect to the system. The Chinese were singled out in the press, but they were no worse than the majority of downtown businesses at the time.[13]

The Chinese-tunnel legend is a popular one and has been extensively examined by historians and folklorists. The demolition phase of Boise's urban renewal project in the early 1970s provided the opportunity to look for any evidence of a tunnel system. None was found, other than small basement extensions used for storage under sidewalks. Tacoma, Pendleton, Nampa, and other Northwest cities have similar legends, but they have no tunnels either.[14] Like all urban tales, this one is too intriguing not to be repeated whether it is true or not. The movies have contributed their bit to our concept of Chinatown as a place of mystery and intrigue, where "hatchet men" of rival tongs appear out of a maze of secret passageways to commit reprisal murders or to kidnap white girls to be sold into slavery in the Orient. *Limehouse Blues*, starring George Raft and Anna May Wong (1934), was typical of movies portraying Chinatown—in this case London's—as a dangerous and sinister place.[15]

Raids on opium dens in Boise increasingly resulted in the arrest of young women. Some were probably prostitutes, but others may have been curious teenagers. Charlie Ling was charged with conducting an opium joint in a shack between Third and Fourth streets and Main and Grove in August of 1901. Anna Smith and Maggie Foster were arrested in his place that month.[16] The Chinese Masonic Hall on Idaho Street was raided regularly for opium smokers, and the officers usually netted a few who were too much under the influence of the drug to avoid arrest. The same addicts and den operators were arrested repeatedly, paid their fines, and continued to smoke. Elaborate care was taken to avoid apprehension, with bunks in hidden rooms where users could recline while the opium took effect. Lookouts were posted to give the alarm if police appeared.[17]

Lawyers who defended those caught in the Masonic Hall raids insisted that their clients were in fact not breaking the city ordinances since they were in their own home when arrested. The *Statesman* commented: "As a matter of fact a great many Chinamen do reside in the building, but it is impossible for the police to segregate actual residents from visitors, and as a result the 'temple' is nothing more than a common opium joint."[18] It was later discovered that one of the upper floors was occupied by Chinese prostitutes, to the disgust of Mayor Moses Alexander, who had only recently praised the Chinese for erecting a substantial brick Masonic building to replace former ramshackle wooden ones.

With the passage of federal legislation to control the use of opiates in patent medicines, commonly available over the counter in the 19th century, U.S. Treasury agents were assigned to assist local officers in dealing with the problem. The 1906 Pure Food and Drug Act required the listing of opiates on medicine labels. In 1909 federal law banned the importation of opium for smoking. Before these laws were passed, medical doctors frequently prescribed opium for a wide range of complaints, and it has been estimated that there were more female addicts in the country than male because of this practice.[19] *Statesman* reporters occasionally toured the Chinese quarters accompanied by police officers. They wrote lurid descriptions that reflect white perceptions of the Chinese at the time. Although filled with racism and outrageously purple prose, the value of this 1884 account is that it was written by an eyewitness.

> Proceeding up Seventh to Idaho Street, the writer, under the guidance of a peace officer, was taken into a small building on the left, before which was displayed the sign "Sing Chung & Co."

This proved to be the most respectable store that we found in the Chinese quarter. Porcelain, china, and Japanese goods filled the shelves. There was some woolens also arranged for sale. The interior of the salesroom was quite clean and quite gaudily decorated after the usual Celestial style. Four or five well dressed Chinamen loitered about in front of the counter and a dude-like salesman poised in fine garb before the rows of goods at the further end. By the front window and behind the counter sat an elderly accountant busily engaged in thumbing a "calculator" and making sundry hieroglyphic insignia upon the pages of a brown-paper book. The few Chinese loafers present spoke in subdued and respectful tones to each other, and it might have been imagined that they had assembled to join in a

Prayer Meeting

or funeral, were it not for the sight of a set of dominoes and the paraphernalia for a game of fan-tan, which was apparently about to begin. Leaving this place, and passing westward along the side of Idaho Street, we passed a small coophole, where the painted, ugly, bloated faces of Celestial women appeared through the door. As we passed these places a nauseating stench was perceptible and all manner of filth was observable on every hand. A little further on is a large wooden building two stories high, in front of which is displayed the words "Bon-Hong." Here in one room about twenty Mongolians were gathered around a large table and playing fan-tan. Several flickering candles illuminated the board and the weird, uncanny faces of the stoical gamesters who lost without murmuring and only betrayed satisfaction when they won, by a dark, sinister smile. Between the two managers of the game sat a Chinese girl, who resembled accurately in face and dress the famous description of an

Oriental Houri

by Thomas W. Knox, the renowned Eastern traveler and author. Her complexion was olive, and no traces of paint were visible. Her eyes, dark and large and mystical, glowed with a peculiar light as she alternately watched the game and gazed motionless and silent at those around her. Upon her high, oval brow was a cap of beads and silk, with gold trimmings, which gave something of barbaric pomp and grotesque beauty to the placid aspect of her immovable wax-like features. A spectator would not have imagined from her passive appearance that she was gambling with the rough and dirty rabble around her, but such was the case. Presently she staked her last dollar on a chance of fortune, and—lost. Then she borrowed from a neighbor, and once more confided to the fickle Goddess of Chance. Every night these scenes are repeated in a dozen different places. Gambling is a natural vice to the Chinese. Passing through a rickety old corridor and ascending a pair of stairs, we came next to a series of bunks, one above another, ranged in such close proximity that a 10-year-old boy could hardly sit up in the space allotted to each bed. In the center of the dark aisle an oil lamp burned dimly, and upon the floor lay two half-stupefied Celestials, taking a last pull at the narcotic pipe. The air in the place was stifling and seemed to exert an unearthly influence over the senses, and as we hastened out into purer atmosphere, a dozen more pallid and emaciated forms seemed to flit by like specters from a Plutonic realm as we passed them, reclining in various positions, within the little bunks, where they had crawled to realize in dreams the gorgeous, lurid wonders of phosphorescent worlds inspired by spirit. Several other dives almost identical with this are more or less patronized here. Eighth to the north side of Idaho Street, we found six other shanties entirely occupied by the Celestials. Most of these places are gambling houses, but there is one opium joint and one drug store.

Now this is the kind of gang that has found a

footing in the midst of our beautiful city. Our Chinatown is only beginning to bear the rank, poisonous, blighting and obnoxious fruits which are sure to ripen into a harvest of crime and disease, if we continue to foster the Celestial dragon right at the door of our very homes.[20]

X

The Chinese Must Go

驅逐

Growing anti-Chinese agitation in California led in 1879 to the passage by Congress of an act to exclude Chinese laborers from entering the United States. The act was vetoed by President Rutherford Hayes because it violated terms of the 1868 Burlingame treaty, which guaranteed Chinese the right to immigrate to the United States but not to attain citizenship.[1] In 1882 a Chinese Exclusion Act was passed, suspending the immigration of Chinese laborers for a period of 10 years, and signed by the president. Laborers already in the country were required to register and receive a certificate listing name, age, occupation, last place of residence, and a personal description. The possession of the certificate allowed Chinese who were in the country before November 17, 1880, to travel to China and be readmitted to the United States.[2]

Agitation against the Chinese, especially in the West, developed into a movement to deport all of the Chinese, whether legally entitled to be in the country or not. The war cry across the West was "The Chinese Must Go." The complaint most often voiced against Chinese laborers was that they drove wages down by their willingness to work for less than white men would. It was claimed that white workers were being denied jobs because the Chinese had a monopoly in certain fields. At the height of the 1885 clamor to drive the Chinese out of Boise, the *Statesman* observed:

> It cannot be denied that the Chinese in our city are important factors in varied fields of labor. First, they are cooks and do nearly all the house work for families who are able to employ domestics. Second, they keep wash houses and do nearly all the washing for the people of the city. Third, they plant gardens and supply the people with vegetables. These are the most important industries, and we must look at the result in a plain and sensible way . . . . sawing wood, sweeping out stores, saloons and other kinds of chores that Chinamen are now employed in can be readily supplied by white labor. But there is, nevertheless, good cause to complain against white labor. The white laborer

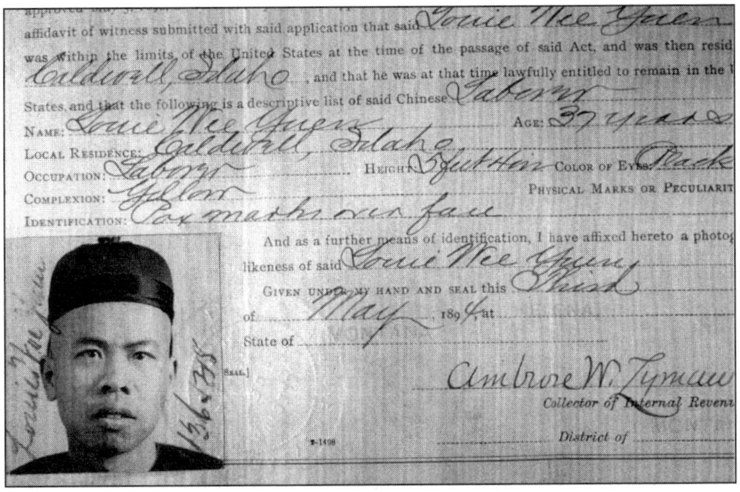
affidavit of witness submitted with said application that said Louie Wee Yuen
was within the limits of the United States at the time of the passage of said Act, and was then resid
Caldwell, Idaho , and that he was at that time lawfully entitled to remain in the
States, and that the following is a descriptive list of said Chinese Laborer
NAME: Louie Wee Yuen AGE: 37 years
LOCAL RESIDENCE: Caldwell, Idaho
OCCUPATION: Laborer HEIGHT: 5 feet 4 in COLOR OF EYES: Black
COMPLEXION: Yellow PHYSICAL MARKS OR PECULIARIT
IDENTIFICATION: Pox marks over face
And as a further means of identification, I have affixed hereto a photo
likeness of said Louie Wee Yuen
GIVEN UNDER MY HAND AND SEAL this Third
of May , 1894, at
State of
[SEAL.]
Ambrose W. Lyman
Collector of Internal Reven
District of

Louie Wee Yuen of Caldwell, like other Chinese in America after the Exclusion Act of 1882 was passed, had to carry a certificate of legal residence showing that he was in the United States before November, 1880. This document was issued to him after renewal of the act in 1892. It indicates that he was born in China in 1857 and came to America when he was 23.
ISHS

> is prodigal in his expenses, and cares as a general rule, very little about saving his earnings.[3]

Attempts to boycott Chinese businesses and those that employed Chinese labor were unsuccessful because the Chinese clearly played a vital economic role in the community, were patient and dedicated workers, and took menial jobs that whites were not willing to perform. It is noteworthy that they did not compete against white labor in other areas.

Violence against the Chinese reached its peak in September, 1885. Five Chinese accused of murdering a white merchant near Pierce City in north Idaho were hanged by a band of white vigilantes.[4] In Green River, Wyoming, an even worse outrage occurred when white miners shot and killed 28 unarmed Chinese miners employed by the same company. More than 500 escaped by rail when Union Pacific conductors were ordered to pick them up and take them to Evanston. At the urging of President Grover Cleveland, Congress eventually appropriated $150,000 to partially compensate the Chinese for the loss of their property. Company houses as well as those of the Chinese had been burned by the mob.[5] In Tacoma, Washington, on November 3, 1885, a mob led by the mayor, the sheriff, the fire chief, a judge, and the head of the Young Men's Christian Association rounded up 200 Chinese and marched them at gunpoint to the railroad station, where they were put on a train to

Portland. Their houses with all their possessions were burned to the ground.[6] In June, 1886, a Chinese laundry was blown up in the Wood River mining town of Broadford. Three laundrymen smelled the burning fuse and narrowly escaped. This incident indicated that there were some in the Wood River country willing to commit murder to get rid of the Chinese, and it led the *Statesman* to criticize the Hailey *News-Miner* for being largely responsible for encouraging and inciting violence: "The *News-Miner* does not offer a word of censure to the would-be-murderers." The *Statesman* thought the *News-Miner* should take "a bold stance in defense of law and order."[7]

Governor Edward A. Stevenson had issued a proclamation a few weeks earlier warning all persons not to molest the Chinese, and he said that those responsible would be prosecuted to the full extent of the law.[8] An anti-Chinese league formed in Boise in 1885 passed resolutions favoring expulsion of the city's Chinese but did not get much support. It never had more than a dozen active members, and the governor's presence in the city discouraged acts of violence by them or anyone else so inclined. This did not mean that the abuse of individual Chinese did not continue, or even that the Governor did not sympathize with those who wanted them to leave, but for the chief executive the maintenance of law and order had a higher priority.[9]

By the 1880s Idaho's Chinese had learned that justice could be had in the courts. Their benevolent societies retained some of the finest lawyers available and did not hesitate to sue if their individual or group interests were violated. The tongs were most often called upon to defend countrymen accused of being illegal aliens under the 1882 Exclusion Act. In 1892 Chinese laborers were excluded for an additional 10 years by the Geary Act. Merchants were not considered laborers, and men previously so classified became partners in businesses of various kinds. There were many who did not register in 1882 or in 1892, and thousands who had entered the country illegally since, often with false papers. The huge discrepancy between official census figures and well-informed estimates of Boise's Chinese population over the years is striking testimony to this.[10]

In 1902 the Exclusion Act was renewed again, this time for an indefinite period. Arrest of illegal aliens was stepped up and deportations increased. U.S. Commissioner Jonas W. Brown, a pioneer lawyer from Idaho City noted for his early prominence in the temperance movement, heard dozens of cases of alleged illegals in 1903. Some, like Sing Ye Mow and Ah Lin, were able to prove that they were born in America of Chinese parents. They were released.[11] Scores of others were escorted by federal officers to Portland or Seattle for deportation to China. In a few cases, even without proper papers, Commissioner Brown was persuaded that a man, like Boise gardener Louie Jan had been in America before 1880 and ordered that certificates of residence be issued to him.[12]

Tens of thousands of Chinese continued to enter the United States by way of Canada or Mexico, often with papers purchased in Hong Kong. This illegal tactic became unnecessary in 1943 when China and the United States were allies in the war against Japan; Congress repealed earlier laws and for the first time granted naturalization rights to foreign-born Chinese.[13]

共濟會

XI

Freemasons

The three-story building in the center of this Idaho Street view is the Chinese Masonic Hall built in 1901 and '02. Chin Man Sui had his herbal medicine shop on the ground floor. The lodge meeting room was on the top floor. City Hall and Boise National Bank are at right at the corner of Eighth Street.
ISHS photo

Boise's largest Chinese association was the Order of Freemasons. Like the other associations (tongs), the Hip Sing, Hop Sing, and Soo Yuen, it was organized as a benevolent and protective society to provide social, recreational, cultural, and legal services for an almost entirely male population that spoke little or no English. The name "Freemason" was chosen to deflect racism and to gain acceptance in the white community as a lodge similar to their own. The Chinese Freemasons had no connection with Euro-American Freemasonry; they traced their beginnings to a tong formed in China more than 300 years earlier in an attempt to overthrow the Manchu Dynasty.[1]

There were Chinese Freemason organizations in the Chinatowns of many cities, including New York and Vancouver, and Lethbridge, Canada. Centerville, Idaho, in the Boise Basin, had a Chinese Masonic Hall that was rented by a white clergyman in 1879 for use as a

清明

CHING MING

church.[2] The Canadian lodges were named Chi Kung Tong and had buildings described as "an interesting cultural mix of East and West" with deeply recessed balconies similar to those common in southeastern China.[3] (Boise's Hop Sing Tong headquarters on Front Street, torn down by urban renewal in 1972, was an example of the style.) The Masonic Order in New York called itself "Long We Tong En Wi," a name translated as "The Order and Brotherhood of Masons." Chinese Freemasons there still publish *The Chinese Republic News*.[4]

Boise crowds were attracted to Idaho Street in the 1890s when the Chinese Masons celebrated religious holidays. Newspaper reports shed little light on the meaning of the events, one account noting only: "They had a grand pow-wow with high priest and roast beef variations."[5] One can deduce what the celebrations were for from the time of year they occurred. Ching Ming, an ancient religious festival held each spring, was probably the one described in the *Idaho Statesman* on March 7, 1901:

> The Chinese joss returned from Idaho City yesterday and the Celestials joined in their annual celebration. The line of march extended down Main Street to Tenth and up Idaho to Seventh, where the celebration was held. The Columbia Band and the Chinese Masons and other Chinese were in the procession. After a lot of noise further proceedings suspended until noon today. It is said $500 worth of firecrackers will be set off during the series of celebrations.[6]

Ching Ming, a spring festival devoted to remembrance of dead ancestors, has been celebrated in China since 3700 B.C. It symbolizes the renewal of life after the death of winter and is a time of planting and looking to "the well-being of one's ancestors," to "ensure the family's prosperity, health and blessings." Sometimes called "tomb sweeping day," Ching Ming is a time to visit cemeteries, to tidy up graves, and to leave offerings of food and drink. "Spirit paper money in gold and silver, and paper drawings and images of necessary items are burned as a way of providing the departed with all their

needs."[7] The Chinese section in Morris Hill Cemetery, at the corner of Emerald and Latah streets, has a small shrine-like furnace still used today for burning paper offerings on Ching Ming and at funerals.[8]

A Boise Chinese, when once asked somewhat scornfully "Just when do you think your dead are going to come and eat that food you are putting on their graves?" replied, "Oh, about the same time your people are going to come and smell those flowers."[9] It was a valid point: in both cases the offerings are symbolic tokens of love, respect, and remembrance.

In 1901 the April festival was chosen for the initiation of 25 new members into the Masonic tong. The *Statesman* reporter enjoyed the spectacle held in front of the Chinese hall at Eleventh and Main but couldn't understand its meaning. "The members themselves won't say a word, and it is said that the initiated themselves *couldn't* say a word for a day or two if they would," he wrote. "Whenever the local Celestials have a high jinks there's excitement on the corner."[10]

In June, 1901, the Masons announced plans to build "a magnificent temple" on Idaho Street between Seventh and Eighth. Architect W.S. Campbell, whose Idanha Hotel had just been completed, was chosen to design a three-story building with retail space on the first floor, sleeping rooms on the second, and a lodge hall and temple on the third. The *Statesman* noted that foreign-born Chinese were prohibited by law from acquiring title to real estate but that Fong Suey, who was agent for purchase of the property was an American-born citizen and could.[11] He bought the lot from brewer and former Mayor John Lemp for $3,800 and was assisted in the project by a $13,000 loan from a local banker.

Chinese merchants Bong Hong & Co., who had occupied a wooden building razed to make way for construction of the temple, planned to take space in the new building, the first substantial brick and stone building built for the Chinese in downtown Boise. The new structure won praise from the public, and detailed reports of construction progress appeared in the news almost daily.

In August, 1902, more than 200 Chinese

Superb works of art decorated the Chinese Masonic Hall and other tong meeting places in the early 20th century. This painting on glass was done from the back side. It represents symbolically what every Chinese family hoped and prayed for: long life, wealth, and children (preferable male heirs).
ISHS collection

Good luck signs like this one adorned lodge halls, temples, gambling houses, and tong meeting places all over Chinatown. This one came from the Hip Sing Tong Building.
Arthur A. Hart photo

Freemasons attended a feast in the new hall honoring the dead on the occasion of Da Jui, the "Hungry Ghost Festival," held yearly on the fifteenth day of the seventh moon in the Chinese lunar calendar. This observance seeks to pacify the ghosts of strangers and un-cared-for dead, whose spirits are believed still present and potentially harmful to the living. Perhaps it is the Chinese equivalent of our Halloween, when "blighted souls seek other souls to take their places in hell." [12]

The Masons celebrated the birth of "Chin Gin Nam, one of the founders of the order" during the Ching Ming festival of the dead in April, 1903.[13]

In 1904 the *Statesman* began editorializing against the new temple, calling it a nuisance. "This 'temple' is the gathering place for the worst elements of the Chinese . . . clean it out. Let the owners use the building for any legitimate purpose, but prevent it from becoming a lodging place for Chinese, or a lounging place for them."[14]

By that time most of Chinatown had moved to an area centered on Front Street and Seventh. In March a petition signed by 28 downtown property owners was presented to the mayor and city council, asking the police to crack down on what had "for a considerable time" been conducted as "an opium joint and for . . . immoral and unlawful purposes."[15] It was widely believed that Chinese prostitutes occupied the second floor rooms, first described as living quarters for members of the order. Yee Wee, interpreter for the Chinese Masons, told the *Statesman*: "The temple is in reality a charitable institution for the Chinese of this section of the country, and was originally planned as an asylum for those who had no means. Every new Chinaman who comes to the city, who is possessed of any means, is asked to pay a fee of $2.50 towards the maintenance of the building. On the other hand, every Chinaman who has no money is privileged to make a bed anywhere in the temple and stay on there until his financial condition improves."[16]

Despite all attempts to close them down, Boise's Chinese Freemasons continued to use their Idaho Street temple until there were no longer enough members left to maintain it. During the Chinese New Year's celebrations in 1912 the Masons marked a new era in the history of their ancient homeland by flying the flag of Dr. Sun Yat Sen's Republic of China.[17]

By the 1930s stories about Chinatown had become nostalgic reminiscences of a colorful part of the city's past. Eva Hunt Dockery shared her memories of the Chinese Masonic Hall:

> The top [third] floor was given over entirely to the lodge room, resplendent in its gold and lacquer shrine, with its pewter candlesticks and punk [sticks] and gay hand embroideries; the second floor was the rooming house of many Chinese; the main floor held a restaurant in the rear, and Dr. Chin Man Sui's drug store in front. In the basement, and probably even below that, were other bunks for sleeping.[18]

This building, the last survivor of the first Chinatown on Idaho Street, was demolished by urban renewal in the 1970s.

XII

Tongs and Tong Wars

堂鬥爭

The Hip Sing Tong hosted the national convention of the association for the third time in 1938. Delegates came from every major Chinatown in America. Governor Barzilla Clark posed with tong officers on the balcony of the Hip Sing Building at 215 ½ Capitol Boulevard on September 10, 1938.
ISHS 71-156.19

The word "tong" in the Cantonese dialect means "hall" or meeting place. In America it came to mean a secret society or association originally formed for benevolent and protective purposes. It later became associated with organized crime. The first such group is believed to have been formed in San Francisco in 1874.[1] The tongs were especially important to newly arrived Chinese men who could not speak English and had little or no money and no friends. The tong might help them find temporary shelter or a job or lend them money for a doctor, a dentist, or an attorney if the need arose.[2]

Many of the tongs were family associations of people with the same surname from the same part of Guangdong. The Soo Yuen family association of Boise, for example, was made up of Louies, Fongs, and

This may have been the last picture taken of the Hip Sing Building before its demolition by Boise's urban renewal agency.
Arthur A. Hart photo, September, 1971

The word "tong" had begun to have bad connotations by the 1920s as big city tongs battled for control of gambling, drugs, and prostitution. Boise's chapter changed its name to "Hip Sing Association."
ISHS 75-104.1

The beautiful Hop Sing Tong Building was on Front Street near Capitol Boulevard, just around the corner from the rival Hip Sing Tong.
Arthur A Hart photo

An elegant carved and gilded window bracket on the Hop Sing Building gives but a faint suggestion of the opulence inside the tong's meeting rooms.
Arthur A. Hart photo

This is the sad ending of Chinatown's handsomest building. It was the last holdout against urban renewal destruction of Chinese buildings at Front and Capitol.
Arthur A. Hart photo

Kwongs.[3] The Chinese Masonic Lodge, discussed elsewhere, was the earliest benevolent and protective association formed in Boise.[4]

The Hip Sing and Hop Sing associations were the most active tongs in Boise in the 20th century, with substantial brick headquarters buildings. Like other Idaho lodges that built their own halls, such as the Odd Fellows and the Masonic orders, the Chinese meeting rooms were on the upper floors and the ground floors were rented out to produce income. In Boise, tenants included shopkeepers, herb doctors, and restaurants.[5]

The Hip Sing Tong was located upstairs at 215½ South Seventh Street in 1921, offering Chinese merchandise downstairs in space later rented to a variety of businesses.[6] This tong was strong enough to host national conventions in 1917, 1927, and 1938 when delegates came from major cities. The business meetings sometimes lasted a week.[7]

By the 1920s, large city tongs were in fierce competition with each other for control of gambling, illegal drugs, and prostitution. As with organized white crime mobs in Chicago and New York, clashes were frequent and marked by murder, extortion, and destruction of property. The words "Tong War" made headlines in the nation's newspapers, reinforcing the common perception that Chinatowns were places of intrigue, crime, and danger.

Even in Boise, if a Hip Sing member was murdered the Hop Sings were suspected of the crime, and before long a Hop Sing would be murdered in retaliation. These slayings were often carried out by "hatchet men" from out of town, so-called because a hatchet was sometimes the weapon used. The hired assassins were also often called "highbinders," a word that came into the English language in the 1870s.[8]

Boise's tongs tried desperately to stay out of these clashes between their counterparts in large cities. When a local tong member was killed, most members of the rival tong went into hiding, fearing that retaliation would come but not knowing who the victim might be. Local officials, usually led by the mayor and police chief, tried to negotiate a peace before a full-scale altercation that might kill dozens could break out. After meetings with representatives of the local Hip Sing and Hop Sing associations, a truce would be worked out and life in Chinatown returned to normal.[9]

Boise never had a branch of the powerful On Leong Tong, which was often at war with the Hip Sing Tong in New York and San Francisco. Violence there spilled over into other cities where there was a local Hip Sing group.[10] The Bing Kong Tong was another national association that sometimes clashed with the Hip Sings, as it did in 1921 in Butte, Montana.[11] The Bing Kongs were once the dominant tong in Seattle and still maintain quarters there. The Hop Sings were dominant in Tacoma.[12] There were local Hop Sing Tongs in Los Angeles and Marysville, California, the first dating from the 1870s.[13]

協勝堂

HIP SING

合勝堂

HOP SING

These wooden markers with their distinctive silhouettes, are labeled with the names of Hop Sing Tong (left) and Soo Yuen Tong, (right). Soo Yuen was a family association. Their use is unknown.
Arthur A. Hart photo

The Los Angeles society is still active, as are the Bing Kong and the Soo Yuen family association.[14] Seattle also has a Soo Yuen association; the group's headquarters are in San Francisco.[15]

Boise got its first taste of tong violence early on the morning of January 16, 1910, when leading merchant Fong Shue was the victim of a murderous attack with hatchets and knives by three members of the Louie family. The attack was believed to be a retaliation on the Fong family for aiding a runaway slave girl from San Francisco. Chen Mory had been brought to Boise in the summer of 1909 by a Silver City laundryman named Wong Gow. They were married by a justice of the peace in Boise soon after they arrived.[16]

Governor James N. Gillett of California asked that Idaho Governor James H. Brady have them arrested and extradited for trial in California on a charge that the girl

Music recorded in Canton in the 1920s made popular listening for the people of Chinatown, and added an exotic touch to the experience of all who passed by. The caption above the phonograph reads "sounds good."
ISHS SG 26/91

had stolen $450 worth of jewelry. Boise Chinese told the governor that they believed the charges were trumped up as a means of getting Chen Mory back in the clutches of the tong that owned her. Local sympathy quickly grew for the young newlyweds. Church groups petitioned the governor not to send the girl back to "a life of sin." Brady listened to the testimony of Chen Mory and Wong Gow, of California officers sent to bring them back, and of a lawyer hired by Boise Chinese before he decided not to allow the extradition and ordered their release.[17]

The case stirred local emotions, exploited to the full by newspaper reporters who saw romance in the fugitive's elopement to escape a vicious San Francisco tong. They referred more and more to "the beautiful Chen Mory" as the helpless victim of evil men and predicted, almost hopefully it seems, that Boise would soon have a full-scale tong war.

"Lives of Local Chinamen in Jeopardy" (October 6, 1909); "Tong War Breaks Out in Boise in Murderous Assault on Local Chinaman" (January 17, 1910): and "War to the Knife is Declared by Warring Factions of Local Chinese." (January 18, 1910).[18] Sensational headlines like these kept public interest high. As a matter of fact, no such war had been declared, and leaders of the Fong and Louie tongs declared a truce–one that eventually led to their joining to form the long-lasting Soo Yuen family association.

A clash between the Hip Sing and Hop Sing tongs in LaGrande, Oregon, in March 1917, resulted in the fatal shooting of a Hip Sing.[19] Boise members of the two organizations again went into hiding, not wishing to be drawn into a war that had started in San Francisco's Chinatown. There had been seven deaths in Portland when police threatened to arrest all Chinese in that city, Astoria, and The Dalles, reputed "headquarters points of Chinese highbinder activity in the northwest."[20]

SOO YUEN

The war hit Boise on March 31 of 1917, when Wong Bock Sing, an elderly laundryman belonging to the Hop Sing tong, was riddled with bullets by hatchetmen of the Hip Sing tong. Wong had been in Boise most of his life, had no known enemies, and was murdered for no other reason than his affiliation with the Hop Sings. Louie Moon, a Boise Hip Sing member, who had served 18 months in the Idaho penitentiary for the murder of Fong Shue in 1909, was one of the first arrested. He had also been picked up in LaGrande after the tong violence there.[21]

When the Wong Bock Sing murder case came to trial in October of 1917, Louie Moon had been released and the defendants were Dong Sing and Lo Ming, also members of the Hip Sing Tong. Prosecutor James H. Hawley, former Boise mayor and Idaho governor, declared that he would show that "the tong war that raged in six western and Pacific coast states last February and March culminated in the murder of the Boise laundryman."[22] Wong Chow, who worked in the laundry, had witnessed the shooting and positively identified the defendants as the ones who had shot his boss. Defense attorneys argued that their clients were someplace else at the time, but after an hour the jury returned a verdict of guilty of murder in the first degree; the defendants were sentenced to life imprisonment.

When another elderly Chinese laundryman from Cascade, Idaho, was beaten and robbed in a Boise alley

The joss house was located at the northeast corner of Capitol Boulevard and Front Street.

in January, 1919, by two Chinese, the *Statesman* again predicted a tong war. The victim was a Hip Sing and his attackers were Hop Sings, but leaders of Boise's two tongs denied that there would be a war over the incident and vowed to let the law take its course.[23] Meetings to solemnize the peace pacts were held in the little temple at Capitol Boulevard and Front Street.

Nineteen thirty-four saw another murder in Chinatown, but leaders of the Hip Sing, Hop Sing, and Soo Yuen societies again signed a solemn agreement not to participate in any tong war, whether initiated inside or outside of Boise. The pact noted: "Trouble would hurt business and be expensive in money as well as lives."[24]

Never again would the city's Chinese community face the threat of a tong war. By 1941, when America entered World War II, little was left of the once thriving Chinese culture that had been a significant part of Boise life. The tongs had so few members that by the 1950s they no longer celebrated traditional holidays except with quiet dinner gatherings of friends and relatives. Nationally, the tongs have continued to battle for control of drugs, gambling, and prostitution. Street gangs of teen-age Chinese have become a major factor in these battles for control in major American cities, and an increasing problem for law enforcement.

XIII

New Chinatown

新唐人街

These Front Street buildings between Capitol Boulevard and Sixth Street, are all that remain of Boise's new Chinatown. They were built on property leased from Harry Parnell. The two-story building was built in 1911 by the Chinese Odd Fellows, later called Hip Sing Tong.
Arthur A. Hart photo

After years of complaints about conditions in the row of flimsy wooden buildings on Idaho Street occupied by Chinese laundrymen, gamblers, merchants, and prostitutes, the City Council condemned the structures as a health hazard on September 20, 1901. "The action of the city authorities with respect to what is called 'Chinatown' is timely," said the *Statesman.* "The nest there in the heart of the city is an eyesore, a disgrace, and a menace to the public health. The buildings are mere shacks, and their surroundings are filthy beyond belief."[1]

A new Chinatown was started at once on Front Street on land leased by the Wah On Company from Harry Parnell, a pioneer butcher. The 99-year lease was for $270 quarterly, with an option to renew or to lease additional land in the same block.[2] As noted earlier foreign-born Chinese could not buy land at the time, but their American-born children could.

The eviction of the Chinese from Idaho Street was accomplished within a matter of days. On September 25, 1901, "The Chinese occupying buildings ordered by the city council to be torn down have been moving, and will probably all be out sometime today. They are generally

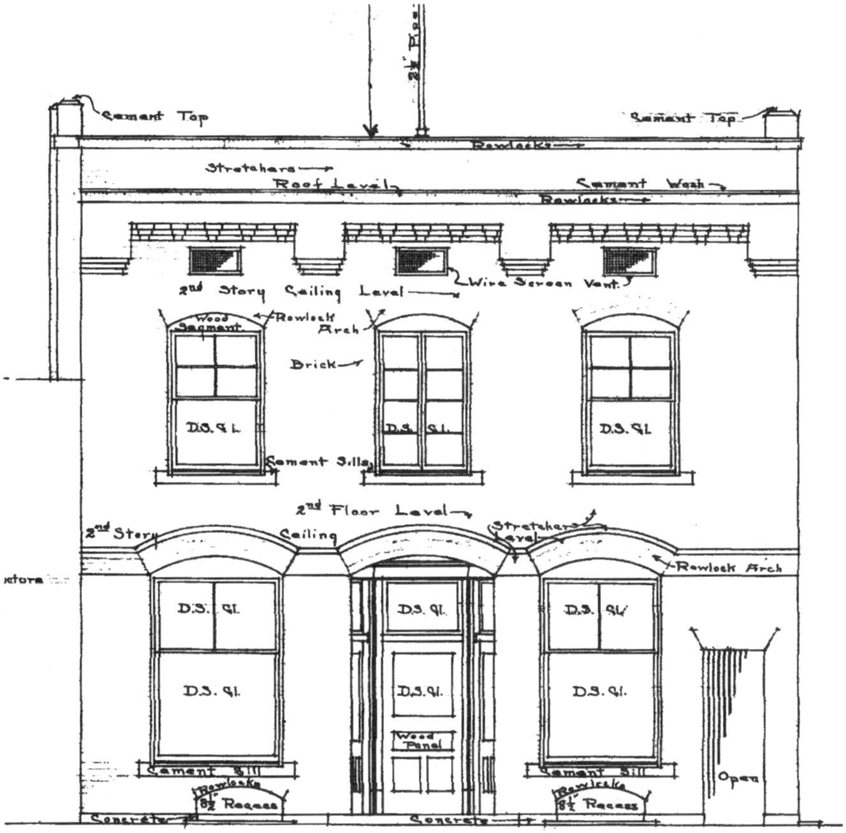

This architectural drawing of the 1911 Chinese Odd Fellows Building is from the archives of Hummel Architects PA, direct descendants of the firm of Tourtellotte & Hummel, architects of the Statehouse, St. John's Cathedral and other landmarks across the state. The ground floor has been modified to accommodate modern windows.
Courtesy Charles F. Hummel, F.A.I.A.

securing quarters with their more fortunate compatriots."[3] By September 28 nearly all of them had moved, and construction of new quarters began.[4] A one-story brick "Chinese mercantile building," designed by architect J.E. Tourtellotte, was completed before the year was out at a cost of $5,000, and another $2,000 worth of construction on the Parnell property was under way. Since new Chinatown was within the fire limits, all construction was supposed to be of brick, although a 30 x 120-foot wooden structure on Sixth Street was allowed for a lodging house. It was ready for occupancy early in November.[5]

By 1904 two Chinese businesses had reopened on the north side of Front Street. They were Fong Lee & Co., Chinese Merchandise, at 614, and Tin Yen Guey, a restaurant, at 622. The rest of the city's Chinese restaurants were still in the heart of town on Main or Idaho Street.[6]

The visit to Boise in August, 1903, by Liang Ch'I-ch'ao, vice president of the Chinese Empire Reform Association, created a great stir in the Chinese community. He was met at the depot on Front Street, a few blocks west of New Chinatown, and escorted in a procession led by the Columbia Band to the Chinese Masonic Hall for a reception, followed by a banquet.[7]

Liang Ch'I-ch'ao was a noted scholar, author, and reformer associated with K'ang Yu-wei, the leading philosopher of the "new text" school of Confucianism which regarded Confucius as a utopian reformer. The two founded a reform newspaper and a reform organization, both quickly suppressed in 1896. Liang and his secretary Pow Chee were on a tour of North America to visit every sizable Chinese community to enlist support for their organization.[8] As a result of this visit Boise Chinese formed a branch of the Chinese Empire Reform Association, and in 1905 the association erected a meeting house at Seventh and Front streets.[9]

Boise's Chinese community was acutely aware of the need for reform in its homeland. The Qing Dynasty was corrupt, weak, and unable to maintain order—especially in Guangdong, where bandits and rival warlords beset peasant farmers already suffering from years when floods or droughts ruined crops and led to widespread starvation. The Taiping Rebellion (1851–1864), a peasant revolt to secure land reform, took 20 million lives. The war with Japan in 1895 had exposed further the weakness of the government. The Boxer Rebellion, 1901, an effort of the "righteous harmonious fists" to drive the "foreign devils" out, led to the murder of Chinese Christians and missionaries and international military intervention.[10]

Over the years Boise Chinese continued to support reform in China. They contributed generously to Dr. Sun Yat Sen's efforts to overthrow the Qing Dynasty and to create the Republic of China. In 1911, just before the lunar New Year, local Chinese men hurried to get their queues cut off as a symbolic gesture that they were no longer subservient to the old regime but progressive in their politics.[11] The queue cutting added new meaning to the age-old practice of starting the new year with a clean slate, all debts paid, and prospects for good fortune and prosperity in the months ahead.

Chinatown in 1900, just before its relocation to Front Street, had its greatest population ever. The census of that year recorded 523, up from only 131 in 1890. This reflects the general exodus of Chinese from nearby Boise County, where 1,225 were counted in 1880, 410 in 1890, 305 in 1900, and only 88 in 1910.[12] In 1908 it was estimated that Boise City had about 400 Chinese,[13] but the census of 1910 recorded only 88.[14] Estimates by local observers were consistently higher than the official census, suggesting that many of Boise's Chinese were illegal and subject to deportation under the Exclusion Acts of 1882, 1892, and 1902; they therefore avoided the census takers. In 1920 Chinatown's population was estimated at about 200, but the official census count was 78.[15] On July 2, 1922, the *Statesman* reported: "The colony at present numbers about 200 souls, fully 100 having returned to China in the past year. There are nine women and 14 children."[16] The official count for 1930 was 67; for 1940, only 40.[17]

Boise's Chinese were staunch supporters of the new Republic of China, founded in 1912 with Dr. Sun Yat Sen as president. They began to fly the new flag and joined the Chinese Nationalist Party, with headquarters in a two-story brick building at 622 Front Street. In 1929 the party moved to 612 Front,where it shared space with a Chinese temple. This arrangement continued until World War II, after which the party and its temple no longer appeared in city directories. After the death of Sun Yat Sen in 1925, leadership of the Nationalist Party (Kuomintang) went to General Chiang Kai-chek. His regime was marked by war against the Chinese Communists and Japan, after that country's invasion and conquest of Manchuria in 1931 and full-scale attack on Shanghai in 1937.[18]

Throughout this period Boise Chinese loyally supported Chiang's regime and sent money for war relief. In

In a gesture of patriotism Boise's Chinese community gathered at the Capitol at the end of World War II in 1945 for a group photograph. The families represented are descendants of pioneers—Fongs, Quongs, Louies, and Yees. Raymond Fong holds the American flag.
Courtesy Yee family

1933 they took special interest in the career of Capt. Fong Jim Yick, a Boise boy who had attended Lincoln School through the eighth grade. He had gone to China and married, then enlisted in the Chinese Army. On one of several return visits to Boise he took flying lessons and received his pilot's license on July 4, 1932. When he returned to China he was commissioned an officer in the air force. His brother, Boise businessman Harry Fong, kept the *Statesman* informed of Jim Yick's advancement in the Chinese Air Force and supplied a photograph of him in uniform that the paper printed on February 5, 1933.[19]

"Boise Chinese Willing to Help Nanking Fight Invasion of Japanese" was the headline on a 1937 story that quoted a number of people who also believed that money sent earlier had been wasted because China had not really fought hard enough. "We in America are tired of sending money just to carry on an argument that doesn't get China anywhere," said one. Another, recognizing that China's vastly superior resources in manpower were not enough, said "If China had more big guns and airplanes, I don't believe Japan would last long."[20] After December 7, 1941, America and its allies would learn how difficult it was to drive Japan out of China, no matter how many guns and airplanes they had.

A stroll through Boise's Chinatown in the 1930s, going west from the corner of Sixth and Front, would take you past the home of Gen Fong at 610; Jimmy Fong, whose story is told above, lived upstairs at 610½. Next on Front Street came the Chinese Nationalist Party and Temple at 612, followed by Mon Wo Ching & Co., Quong On Chong Co., Hong Yick Jan & Co., the Soo Yuen family association, and the Chinese Joss House on the corner of Capitol Boulevard. Across the street was the Hai Yuen & Co., Chinese Merchandise, and upstairs, the Hop Sing Tong. If you turned up Capitol and headed north you would come to the locally popular Shang Hai Low Restaurant and the Hip Sing Tong headquarters. Next door was the Wing Hop Wo Co., Chinese Merchandise, and upstairs the herbal medicine store of Herbert Ah Fong. Harry Fong ran the Kwon Hip Yuen & Co. Chinese store. Harry's Bamboo Garden Restaurant was at 108 Capitol Boulevard, just south of Main Street.[21]

In 1934 a Chinese Odd Fellows Hall is listed at 610½ Front, but it does not appear thereafter. The lodge had commissioned architects Tourtellotte and Hummel to design the building in 1911. Company records list the address as 610–612. This is probably the building occupied today by the American Cleaning Company, now numbered 616 Front Street. The Chinese Odd Fellows had no connection with the Independent Order of Odd Fellows, an international fraternal organization founded in 1795. A 1917 *Statesman* story states: "For a number of years the Hip Sing Tong, which has its headquarters upstairs on South Seventh Street, was known as the Odd Fellows' society of the Chinese." The Soo Yuen Club, the family association of the Fongs, Louies, and Kwongs, organized in 1909, had quarters at 622 Front Street that year, and would continue at that location through 1943. By that time the rest of the buildings in the block were vacant, and the little joss house on the corner of Capitol had been torn down. Around the corner at 216 still lived descendants of Harry Parnell, who had leased land in the block to the Chinese in 1901. They were there until the 1950s.[22]

Boise's urban renewal project demolished all of the buildings in the city block bounded by Capitol and Eighth, and Front and Grove in the 1970s. This included the Hip Sing and Hop Sing buildings. The Hop Sing Building on Front Street was the last to go, since the Hop Sings fought the taking of their property in the courts. The plight of aged Billy Fong, who still lived in the building, attracted considerable public sympathy after a story by *Statesman* reporter Tim Woodward quoted Boise Redevelopment Agency board member Charles Newhouse: "He'll leave. Wait'll they swing the iron ball a few times. He'll break a few track records getting outta there."[23] Indignant letters to the editor poured in to the *Statesman* protesting such insensitive comments. Unfortunately, Newhouse's comments reflected quite accurately the agency's attitude at the time about preserving any of the city's architectural or ethnic heritage.

There are three former Chinese buildings left standing on property leased from Harry Parnell in 1901. They are located at 211 South Sixth Street and at 616 Front Street where two of them share one street number. Chinatown lives only in memory, but the city's Chinese heritage lives on through the contributions of today's Chinese Americans.

BOISE CHINESE CELEBRATION DRAWS WIDE INTEREST

云、本縣加關租吏、現據各社團報告、謂
本縣各地、仍有賭館開設、賭風尚未止
息、故派員再行查究賭博、雖日前撥出公
款五千元、專爲查究賭博之用、經查出有
賭館兩間、陳設賭具機器、爲數甚多、但
承法官以在其所管轄之界內、僅得賭館
一家、前曾調查明白、確無違禁物品云、

⊙貝市協勝公會春宴之慶鬧　埃地賀

省貝市埠訊、本埠協勝公會、于夏曆初
八日、設席公會禮堂、舉行春宴、請西賓
五十餘名、俱是省長公署、縣公署、市政
廳、上級官員　及本埠大實業家、報界等
名望領袖、下午八時入席、由市即市文報
總編輯抵溫乞、及公會外交主任鄺光策
君爲主席、抵溫乞搖鈴起立、舉杯與衆共
浮一大白、次光策君起立舉杯敬酒一杯
於省長路市、并祝前途發達、再敬酒一杯
于市長休亞、并祝身體康健、進餐後、酒
及半、抵溫乞起立宣佈旨趣、并介紹公
會正副主席林舉賢、鄺修文二君演說、
由鄺光達傳譯、鄺光策君致歡迎西友詞、
次請省長、司法長、民政長、大理分院法
官、市長、縣承法吏、警察長等、相繼演說
、聞該會近三年來、春宴西賓、俱用唐餐
及中國碗碟筷子等　情形熱鬧、至十二時
許、燃放炮竹、賓主乃盡歡而散、

●屋崙華僑團體會通告

爲通告事照得本會決議召集全僑大會籌

Pictured here is a Chinese newspaper account of the Chinese New Year party in Boise, at which city, county, and state officials were guests of the Hop Sing Tong. The story appeared in the *Chinese World*, published in San Francisco, and was written by Henry Fong, Boise correspondent for the San Francisco publication.

Notes

I
The Chinese Come to Idaho

1 *Idaho Tri-weekly Statesman*, (Boise), September 14, 1865.
2 Mike Hanley and Ellis Lucia, *Owyhee Trails: The West's Forgotten Corner* (Caldwell, Idaho: Caxton Printers, 1974), 212.
3 *Oregonian* (Portland), February 17, 1865.
4 *Oregonian*, March 1, 1865.
5 *Idaho World*, (Idaho City) September 30, 1865.
6 Mark Twain, *Roughing It* (1875), Volume II, Chapter XIII, 135.
7 *Idaho Tri-weekly Statesman*, April 7, 1877.
8 U.S. Department of Commerce, Bureau of the Census, *Ninth Census of the United States* (1870) through *Fourteenth Census of the United States* (1920).

II
Religion

1 *Chinese Cultural Studies: Philosophy and Religion in China*, Compton's Living Encyclopedia on America Online (August 1995) http://www.academic.brooklyn.cuny.edu/core9/phalsall/texts/chinrelg.html.
2 Ibid.

3 The author has citations for nearly 100 cases of harassment of the Chinese in Boise, ranging from pranks to beatings and destruction of property. Murders of Chinese in the city in the century treated by this book were, with but one exception, by other Chinese. Some were related to wars between tongs, but most were over gambling. Chinese were sometimes beaten and robbed by other Chinese badmen as well.

4 *Idaho Statesman* February 5, 1919, February 27, 1919, March 10, 1919. A "Joint Americanization Committee," sponsored by local churches was active in Boise for several years. It helped Chinese learn English, and was popular as a social club.

5 *Chinese Cultural Studies* loc. cit.

6 *Confucius, K'ung-fu-tzu* http://www.friesian.com/confuci.html, p 2 of 9.

7 A complete description of the calculations necessary to compute the Chinese lunar year takes five internet pages. For those mathematically inclined, have at it.

8 Many sources are available on the internet on Chinese New Year celebrations worldwide. Good accounts of Boise New Year's celebrations can be found in the following places: *Idaho Tri-weekly Statesman*, February 1, 1870, January 18, 1875.

9 Ibid., February 13, 1877.

10 *Idaho World*, February 20, 1885.

11 *Idaho Statesman*, January 19, 1890.

12 Ibid., February 11, 1899.

13 Ibid. February 18, 1901.

14 Ibid., February 20, 1901.

15 Ibid., February 13, 1911.

16 Ibid., February 17, 1912.

17 Ibid., February 24, 1926.

18 Ibid., February, 1930.

III

Temples

1 Eva Hunt Dockery, *Idaho Statesman*, January 1, 1933.

2 *Webster's Ninth New Collegiate Dictionary* (Springfield, MA, 1984).

3 *Idaho Statesman*, June 21, 1901.

4 Ibid., April 8, 1917.

5 Ibid.

6 Harold Rhodenbaugh, "Chin Law Guan, Soothsayer," *Idaho Statesman*, January 26, 1930.

7 A Chinese visitor to the Idaho Historical Museum in 1973 translated the inscriptions on the temple carvings. They were made in Guangdong in 1885.

8 Rhodenbaugh, loc.cit.

9 "Harvest Festival," *West Shore* (October 12, 1889). 139, 140.

10 Eva Hunt Dockery, "Glory of Chinatown Fades As Men Demolish Joss House," *Idaho Statesman*, March 17, 1937.

11 *Idaho Statesman*, December 25, 1937.

12 This man was known by several of our Chinese informants, but none, 20 years later, could remember his name.

IV
Christians

1 Andrew Gosling, "Religion and Rebellion in China: the London Missionary Society Collection," *National Library of Australia News*, (July 1998), 3–6.

2 *The People of Canton Against the English, 1842,* Internet Modern History Sourcebook, http://www.fordham.edu/halsall/mod/1842canton.html.

3 *Idaho Tri-weekly Statesman*, April 29, 1876.

4 Ibid., July 31, 1869.

5 Ibid., May 25, 1872.

6 Ibid., June 28, 1881. A Chinese American Missionary society was formed in Los Angeles in 1876 and a Chinese Methodist Mission in 1877. A Chinese Congregational Mission was established there in 1888. See *Chinese Americans In Los Angeles*, http://www.camla.org/history/timeline.html.

7 *Idaho Statesman*, December 27, 1904, December 28, 1904.

8 Andy Louie interview with the author, May 22, 2002.

9 *Idaho Statesman*, November 20, 1927.

10 William Quong, interview with the author, May 30, 2002; Faye Yee (widow of Yick Yee), interview with the author, July 3, 2002; Mabel Quong, interview with Jackie Day-Ames, April 27, 29, 1976.

V

Laundrymen

1 *Idaho World*, October 7, 1865.
2 *Ninth Census of the United States* (1870) 351.
3 *Idaho World*, January 20, 1866.
4 *Idaho Tri-weekly Statesman*, October 9, 1875.
5 Ibid., August 23, 1881.
6 Ibid., January 25, 1877.
7 Ibid., August 23, 1881.
8 *Idaho Statesman*, October 6, 1892.
9 Ibid., August 19, 1893.
10 *Idaho Statesman*, September 26, 1893.
11 Ibid., January 10, 1901.
12 Ibid., June 7, 1901.
13 Ibid., May 3, 1901.
14 Ibid., April 5, 1901.
15 *R.L. Polk & Co.'s Boise and Ada County Directory*, 1906, 498.
16 Ibid. 1921, 85.
17 Ibid.
18 Ibid., 1925, 385.
19 *Idaho Statesman*, September 13, 1925.
20 *Polk*, 1934–35, 384.

VI

Gardeners

1 *Idaho Tri-weekly Statesman*, April 11, 1871.
2 Ibid., July 20, 1871.
3 William Quong interview, May 30, 2002.
4 *Idaho World*, May 13, 1869.
5 *Idaho Statesman*, December 5, 1890.
6 Ibid.
7 *Idaho Statesman*, June 18, 1892.
8 Ibid.
9 *Idaho Statesman*, May 22, 1902.
10 Ibid., May 3, 1917.
11 Louie interview, May 22, 2002. The author's father moved his family to farms in Oregon and Washington during the Great Depression of the 1930s, and this passage is based on personal experience.
12 Louie interview.
13 James H. Hawley, *History of Idaho*, 4 vols. (Chicago: S.T. Clark Publishing Co., 1920), II, 45.

14 Louie interview.

VII
Cooks and Cooking

1 Arthur A. Hart, *The Boiseans at Home*, (Boise, Idaho: Historic Boise, 1984), 8, 9.
2 *Ninth Census of the United States*, (1870).
3 *Idaho Tri-weekly Statesman*, August 8, 1876.
4 Ibid., February 28, 1885.
5 *Polk*, 1906–07, 512.
6 *Idaho Statesman*, May 2, 1903.
7 Ibid., April 2, 1890.
8 Ibid., July 9, 1892.
9 Ibid., January 3, 1893.
10 Ibid., December 17, 1893.
11 "Chop Suey Was Invented, Fact or Fiction? August 29, 1896." *Library of Congress* online, http://www.americaslibrary.gov/pages/jb-0829-suey-3.html, 1–3.
12 Ibid., December 28, 1893.
13 Ibid., February 19, 1903.
14 Ibid., September 17, 1904.
15 Ibid., January 2, 1894; *Polk*, 1905, 379; *Polk*, 1906–07, 512.
16 *Idaho Statesman*, August 18, 1908.
17 *Polk*, 1909–10, 560.
18 *Idaho Statesman*, September 24, 1924.
19 Ibid.
20 *Idaho Statesman*, April 30, 1926.
21 Ibid., September 21, 1927.
22 *Polk*, 1939–40, 1950.
23 *Polk*, 1984

VIII
Doctors

1 Hawley, James H., *History of Idaho*, 3:379, Dr. Ah Fong's biography is the only one of a Chinese person in this four-volume work.
2 *Boise City Directory*, 1893.
3 *Polk*, 1904, 52.
4 *Idaho Statesman*, August 31, 1893.
5 Ibid., September 13–14, 1893.
6 Ibid., September 13, 1894.

7 *Idaho Tri-weekly Statesman*, February 19, 1887. (The full text of the act included).

8 *Idaho Statesman*, August 18, 1893, September 5, 1893.

9 Ibid., September 29, 1916.

10 Ibid., August 1, 1899.

11 Ibid., May 24, 1914.

12 Ibid., September 19, 1914.

13 Ibid., May 24, 1914.

14 Charles L. Raymond, L.Ac., conversation with the author, June 13, 2002; Liu Ruimin, conversation with the author, March 27, 2002.

15 *Idaho Statesman*, February 22, 1901.

16 Ibid., March 3, 1904.

17 A.Y. Leung, *Chinese Medicinals*, (Portland, Oregon, 1990), 1–19 See also *Chinese Medicine*, at http://www.gio.gov.tw/info/culture/culture1.html.

18 Dick Ah Fong, conversation with the author, May 21, 2002.

19 *Idaho Statesman*, August 22, 1920.

20 Ah Fong conversation.

21 *Idaho Statesman*, November 1, 1932. Funeral home records indicate that Wing Lee was a "paper name," acquired to gain illegal entry into the United States because of the Chinese Exclusion Acts still in place. His real name was Jung Quong.

22 Family history compiled by Jane Yee, sent to author, June, 2002. (Dick Ah Fong says the Ah Fong doctors also used pulse reading for diagnosis, and that as a child he watched his father use the technique).

23 Faye Yee interview.

24 Summers Funeral Home records in Idaho State Historical Society Library and Archives.

25 Grant Yee, conversation with the author, June 24, 2002.

26 Yee history.

27 *Idaho Statesman*, December 19, 1971.

28 Ibid., January 12, 1973, Yee History.

29 Raymond conversation.

30 Ron Hodge, associate executive director, Idaho Medical Association, conversation with the author; Vicki Vosburg, (herbalist), conversation with the author.

IX
Opium Dens

1 David Courtwright, "Opiate Addiction in the American West," *Journal of the West*, July, 1982, 24.
2 Paul Chrastina, "Emperor of China Declares War on Drugs," Old News. http://www.oldnewspublishing.com/opium.html.
3 *Idaho Tri-weekly Statesman*, June 22, 1874.
4 Ibid., June 28, 1870.
5 Ibid., January 25, 1868.
6 *Idaho World*, July 29, 1879.
7 General Laws of Idaho, 11th Session, January 22, 1881.
8 *Idaho Tri-weekly Statesman*, February 15, 1881.
9 Ibid., August 2, 1883.
10 *Idaho Statesman*, March 27, 1895.
11 Ibid., June 11, 12, 1898.
12 Ibid., October 13, 14, 1888.
13 Ibid., February 6, 1893.
14 Phyllis A. Harrison-Brose, "Validation Through Explanation: Tacoma's Chinese Tunnels," in *Northwest Folklore*, vol. 4, No. 2, (Winter-Spring, 1986). See the web sites of cities listed. The Chinese tunnel myth is now actively exploited by several Western cities to attract tourists to what are only connected basement rooms.
15 I saw this film when it was released by Paramount in 1934; *I* certainly found it sinister.
16 *Idaho Statesman*, August 30, 1901.
17 *Idaho Tri-weekly Statesman*, April 7, 1881.
18 *Idaho Statesman*, March 18, 1904.
19 Courtwright, "Opiate Addiction,".
20 *Idaho Tri-weekly Statesman*, September 25, 1884.

X
The Chinese Must Go

1 *EncyclopediaBrittannica*onlinefile://c:/Program Files/Brittannica/BCD\Cache\-2-ArticleRil.html.
2 Forty-Seventh Congress. Session I. 1882.
3 *Idaho Tri-weekly Statesman*, December 31, 1885.
4 Kenneth Owens. "Pierce City Incident, 1885–1886," *Idaho Yesterdays* 3 (Fall 1959): 8–13.
5 Sucheng Chan. *Asian Americans: An Interpretive*

History (New York: Twayne Publishers, 1991), quoted at http://www.itp.berkeley.edu/asam121/rocksprings.html.

6 Murray Morgan, *Puget's Sound* (Seattle, University of Washington Press, 1979), 212–252.

7 *Idaho Tri-weekly Statesman*, June 29, 1886.

8 Ibid.

9 *Idaho Statesman*, January 26, 1886.

10 Rose H. Lee, "The Growth and Decline of Chinese Communities in the Rocky Mountain Region" (Ph.D. dissertation, University of Chicago, 1947), published in *The Annals of the Chinese Historical Society of the Pacific Northwest* 2, 1983, 256; *Tenth Census of the United States* (1880) through *Twelfth Census of the United States* (1910).

11 *Idaho Statesman*, March 22, 1903, September 2, 1903.

12 Ibid., March 29, 1903, May 12, 1903.

13 Web Page of the Chinese American Museum in Los Angeles, http://www.camla.org/history/timeline.html.

XI
Freemasons

1 Bruce Edward Hall, *Tea That Burns: A Family Memoir of Chinatown* (New York: Free Press, 1997) 203.

2 *Idaho World*, June 27, 1879.

3 Chinatown: Vancouver's unique heritage neighborhood, 1,2, http://www:aibd.bc.ca/publicarchtours/chinatown.html; "The urban Landscape of Downtown Lethbridge, University of Lethbridge Department of Geography, 2.

4 Hall, *Tea that Burns*, 59

5 *Idaho Statesman*, September 5, 1893.

6 Ibid., March 7, 1901.

7 Chinese Historical & Cultural Project, KQED Center for Education and Lifelong Learning (website).

8 Andy Louie, telephone conversation with the author, June 12, 2002.

9 A local story told to the author on several occasions.

10 *Idaho Statesman*, April 2, 1901, June 21, 1902.

11 Ibid., July 13, 1901.

12 Ibid., August 28, 1902.

13 Ibid., April 18, 1903.

14 Ibid., March 18, 1904.
15 Ibid., February 7, 1904.
16 Ibid., undated clipping.
17 Ibid., February 17, 1912.
18 Ibid., January 1, 1933.

XII
Tongs and Tong Wars

1 Boo How Doy, The Early History of Tongs in New York, http://www.organizedcrime.about.comlibraryweeklyaao62401a.html.
2 Mark Higgins, "Old Associations Hold Little Appeal for New Generations," *Seattle Post-Intelligencer*, undated clipping, ca. 1998.
3 The Kwong family should not be confused with the Boise family of Louie Quong. In Chinese the surname comes first, hence Louie Quong, if Americanized, should be Quong Louie. Indeed it was sometimes written that way, but the family finally tired of explaining it and accepted Quong as a surname.
4 Ibid.
5 *Polk*, 1921, 173.
6 Ibid.
7 *Idaho Statesman*, September 4, 1927; *Boise Capital News*, September 18, 1938.
8 See the *Oxford English Dictionary* for a more detailed etymology.
9 *Idaho Statesman*, March 17; April 2; October 15, 1917; January 20, August 28, 1925.
10 Jerry Capeci and Ying Chan, "Ghost Shadow Bosses Betray Members," *New York Daily News*, October 26, 1996. James Dubro, *Dragons of Crime, Inside the Asian Underworld*, Toronto (Octopus Publishing Company, 1992).
11 Tong Wars: Fighting for Family Values in Butte, Montana, http://www.montana.com/maiwah/tong.html.
12 Higgins, "Old Associations."
13 Old Marysville Chinatown, http://www.bokkaitemple.org/IntroductionP4.html; *Chinese Americans in Los Angeles: a Timeline*, The Chinese American Museum in Los Angeles, http://www.camla.org/history/timeline.html.

14 Ibid.
15 Mark Higgins, “”Old Associations.”
16 *Idaho Statesman*, August 17, 1909.
17 Ibid., August 26, September 18, 20, October 10, 1909, January 20, 26, 27, 29, February 3, 1910.
18 Ibid., October 6, 1909, January 17, 18, 1910.
19 Ibid., March 17, 1917.
20 Ibid., March 29, 1917.
21 Ibid., April l, 1917.
22 Ibid., October 7, 1917.
23 Ibid., January 20, 1919.
24 Ibid., April 25, 1934.

XIII
New Chinatown
1 *Idaho Statesman*, September 21, 1901.
2 Ibid., November 9, 1901.
3 Ibid., September 25, 1901.
4 Ibid., September 28, 1901.
5 Ibid., January 1, 1902.
6 *Farr & Smith, Boise City Directory*, 1901–2, 209.
7 *Idaho Statesman*, August 25, 1903. *Evening Capital News*, August 24, 1903.
8 Jung-pang Lo, “Chinese Reform in Idaho,” *Idaho Yesterdays*, 5 (Fall 1961), 20, 21.
9 *Idaho Statesman*, November 14, 1905.
10 Ibid., January 20, 1911.
11 Rose H. Lee, “The Growth and Decline of Chinese Communities in the Rocky Mountain Region.” Ph.D. dissertation (Sociology, 1947) University of Chicago. Published in *The Annals of the Chinese Historical Society of the Pacific Northwest*, II, 256. Bureau of the Census, 1880–1910.
13 *Idaho Statesman*, February 15, 1908.
14 *Tenth Census of the United States*, 1910.
15 *Twelfth Census of the United States*, 1920.
16 *Idaho Statesman*, July 2, 1920.
17 *Thirteenth and Fourteenth Census of the United States*, (1930, 1940).
18 *Polk*, 1921, 431; 1925, 79; 1927, 1929, 1930–31, et.al.
19 *Idaho Statesman*, February 5, 1933.
20 Ibid., August 6, 1937.

21 *Polk* directories.

22 Ibid.

23 *Idaho Statesman*, June 14, 1972.

Suggested Reading

Bancroft, Hubert H. *History of Washington, Idaho, and Montana, 1885–1889.* San Francisco: The History Company, 1890.

Barth, Gunther Paul. *Bitter Strength: A History of the Chinese in the United States, 1850–1870.* Cambridge, Massachusetts: Harvard University Press, 1964.

Daniels, Roger. *Asian America: Chinese and Japanese in the United States Since 1850.* Seattle: University of Washington Press, 1988.

Donaldson, Thomas Corwin. *Idaho of Yesterday.* Caldwell, Idaho: Caxton Printers, 1941.

Elsensohn, Alfreda. *Idaho Chinese Lore.* Cottonwood: Idaho Corporation of Benedictine Sisters, 1979.

Hanley, Mike, and Ellis Lucia. *Owyhee Trails: The West's Forgotten Corner.* Caldwell, Idaho; Caxton Printers, 1974.

Hart, Arthur A. *Basin of Gold: Life in Boise Basin, 1862–1890.* Idaho City: Idaho City Historical Foundation/Historic Idaho, 1987.

Hawley, James H. *History of Idaho.* Chicago: S.T. Clark Publishing, 1920.

Hsu, Francis L.K. *The Challenge of the American Dream: The Chinese in the United States.* Belmont, California: Wadsworth Publishing, 1971.

Schwantes, Carlos A. *In Mountain Shadows: A History of Idaho.* Lincoln: University of Nebraska Press, 1991.

Sung, Betty Lee. *Mountain of Gold: The Story of the Chinese in America.* New York: Macmillan, 1967.

Tsai, Shih-Shan Henry. *The Chinese Experience in America.* Bloomington: Indiana University Press, 1986.

Twain, Mark. *Roughing It.* Hartford, Connecticut: American Publishing, 1872.

Wegars, Priscilla, ed. *Hidden Heritage: Historical Archaeology of the Overseas Chinese.* Amityville, New York: Baywood Publishing, 1993.

Wells, Merle W. *Boise: An Illustrated History.* Woodland Hill, Washington: Windsor Publications, 1982.

____ . *Gold Camps and Silver Cities: Nineteenth Century Mining in Central and Southern Idaho*, 2d ed. Moscow: Idaho Department of Lands, Bureau of Mines and Geology, 1983.

Zhu, Liping. *A Chinaman's Chance.* Niwot, Colorado: University Press of Colorado, 1997.

Index

Other books by Arthur A. Hart

Historic Boise	$10.95
The Boiseans: At Home	$10.95
Basin of Gold: Life in Boise Basin, 1862–1890	$10.95
Life in Old Boise	$27.50
Camera Eye on Idaho: Pioneer Photography, 1863–1913	$24.95
Wings Over Idaho: An Aviation History	$22.95
Boise Baseball: The First 125 Years	$14.95
Barns of the West: A Vanishing Legacy	$29.95
To Protect and to Serve: A History of the Boise Police Department, 1863–2000	$29.95